THE STATELY GAME

THE STATELY GAME

JAMES W. SYMINGTON

The Macmillan Company, New York, New York

Collier-Macmillan Limited, London

THE AUTHOR GRATEFULLY ACKNOWLEDGES:

Américas, for material in Chapter Nine, Part Two, which is adapted from an article printed in the March 1968 issue of *Américas,* monthly magazine published by the Organization of American States in English, Spanish, and Portuguese.

The Reporter, for material in Chapter Six, Part Two, which originally appeared in "Youth, Crime, and the Great Society," published in their February 24, 1966, issue. Copyright 1966 by The Reporter Magazine Company.

The Macmillan Company
866 Third Avenue, New York, N.Y. 10022
Collier-Macmillan Canada Ltd., Toronto, Ontario

Library of Congress Catalog Card Number: 75-138032

First Printing

Printed in the United States of America

TO FRANK AND HELEN BOYDEN
DEERFIELD ACADEMY, DEERFIELD,
MASSACHUSETTS

IT TAKES TIME TO KNOW A COUNTRY

It takes time to know a country,
Time to see the land,
Time to meet the people,
And time to understand,

Time to know your neighbor
On the other side,
Time to learn to labor
In the vineyard of his pride,

Time to watch the reaping,
Tell the wheat from chaff,
Find the reaper weeping,
And learn what makes him laugh.

For this great road we're walking
Has many a pit and bend,
And who can tell for certain
Just where the road will end?

We know it's full of danger
So walk it hand in hand.
It takes time to know a country
And time to understand.

J. W. S.

INTRODUCTION

"Meeting and greeting" is one trivial name for the ancient and serious game of protocol, a game played under rules that maximize the appearance if not the substance of welcome and friendship between nations. This term, one realizes, is understandable since protocol, the largely uncodified system of practices governing diplomatic conduct, is designed to enable enemies to meet as gracefully as friends. As this perforce implies a minimum of candid contact in a context of maximum correctness, even friends are invited to meet along the lowest common denominator of communication-ritual. Yet history reveals that the courtly codes and ceremonies by which sovereigns have dealt with one another over the centuries have failed to provide successful opportunities for the kind of understanding and restraint that render war a mutually unacceptable alternative to further conversation. Somehow the untamed in man, caged in opposite and clashing cultures, has found too few crumbs under the conference tables to satisfy his hunger for freedom, security, *lebensraum*. The bemused contempt, therefore, in which protocol is often held is only the reflection of an acquired skepticism. People have come to doubt both the ability and the commitment of history's parade of presidents, premiers, and

kings, attended by a continuum of timeserving bureau-
crats, to build a better world. The superficial assurances
expressed in ritual, and the bland joint communiques
that emerge from "candid conversations," have lost even
their temporarily hypnotic effect. The public generally
isn't even disappointed, only bored, by the game statesmen play.

The first generation to perceive the full outlines of the
credibility gap in international affairs is not likely to
believe it can be closed by ceremony. Somehow the tender
and elusive agencies of human nature that make for tolerance, and compromise, have not been brought into play
at state levels by the old diplomacy. The world needs a
new diplomacy involving us all. Diplomacy in the
nuclear/jet age is too important to be left to diplomats,
much less to the sovereigns who employ them. It is
people's work.

It is not that the day of the professional diplomat is
over. Far from it. In a world riven by vividly remembered
horrors and indignities, religious scars, distrust between
social systems, and keen competition for military and
commercial advantage, there is plenty to challenge professional competence in the field of diplomacy. But if
diplomacy is the creative art of moving the world to
peace, clearly the task belongs to us all. From experience
and observation I have no doubt that the work of professional diplomacy would be enhanced by a heightened
sensitivity in the average citizen to the consequences of
his behavior. In Rome, for example, busloads of American
tourists are carefully urged not to snap flash cameras in
the Sistine Chapel; the repeated intensification of light
dims the colors of Michelangelo's heroic work. But to
people who are going to "get" what they "paid for," this

request is a fatuous imposition, and many a proud tourist returns with the forbidden snapshot, caring as little about Italian reaction as about the desecration of a shrine of human excellence.

The American service man's family which lives behind the cosmetic curtain, where the PX marks the spot; the businessman abroad who haunts the American bar for years rather than take on a new language in a new setting; the junketeering conventioneer; yes, at times, the congressman who loudly "discovers" inconvenience, uncleanliness, and inefficiency abroad (as if he didn't live with them at home)—none of these gentle people serves the cause of diplomacy. Many of us, like certain unfortunate wines, don't "travel well." No country produces the perfect guest or host, but I speak of Americans because I think our responsibilities in this regard are proportionate to our opportunities—which are unparalleled.

Our opportunities to "meet" begin at home. But this is an effort many avoid because of the cross-cultural demands it entails. Progress and success, as measured here, require only the achievement of certain traditionally remunerative skills and a kind of lubricating politeness to render our contacts and transactions pleasant—or at least tolerable. Our satisfactions in a general way do not depend on sensitivity to others, or on easy, joyous comradeship except in select groupings, or on appreciation of beauty per se as distinct from achievement. We expect our President certainly to represent us at our best. But we feel no compulsion to make his job easier by *being* our best.

When heads of governments meet to reduce tensions and resolve differences, their work to be useful requires the active support of the citizens they serve. The American President, for example, in this decade probably personally meets at least one-third of all the other world leaders every year. His credibility on these occasions, in terms of projecting our desire for "peace with justice," etc., depends in no small part on the background noises we make. But a people who have not met themselves cannot credibly meet others. Nor can anyone, from ambassador to President, do it for them.

There are also unfortunate failures to meet at the top. Such passing concealments as the "Thai contingency plan," our Laotian "commitment," the Philippine "volunteers," and the Cambodian incursion, which caught by surprise fewer VC than MC (Members of Congress), arise from breakdowns in communication between both elected and appointed officials, patriots of generally similar backgrounds but with acquired institutional biases, which cause them to differ occasionally on the need to be truthful with one another and with us all. They don't always "meet" effectively because they share power and this has sharpened their mutual distrust. This happens in the bureaucracy of every system, but should be more vulnerable to challenge in ours.

For entire peoples to live in psychological isolation from each other, however, is a graver problem. It is principally a problem between nations, but some nations have it to an acute degree within their own borders. America belongs in this category, but India, Russia, Nigeria, Belgium, Cyprus, some Latin American countries, and many others should also be included. When a nation's boundaries are determined by historical accident, conquest, the dissolution of empires, or sudden de-colonization, awkward accommodations must be made among former strangers finding themselves under one flag. Millions of odd-lot countrymen eddy in the wake of the oceanic changes that partitioned their old world. Evidently, ethnic and cultural habits and attitudes are not dissolved overnight by immersion in any one national pool. People tend to seek out their "own kind," and form assumptions about the "others," which are often as inaccurate as they are convenient.

America is such a nation. America, through freedom on the one hand and slavery on the other, has brought into one political family people from every corner of the earth, a unique experiment. And what a fateful opportunity to prove that throughout the human race there is more to unite than divide, that diversity need not mean conflict, nor compromise and unity, decay. This is our mission, nobler and more difficult to achieve than the moon landing. We are as close to performing it before this doubting world and our doubting selves as we were to the moon before Robert H. Goddard fashioned his first rocket. But we have the resources to accomplish it, because we have the people. The people are both lock and key, problem and solution, illness and antidote. When the many-blooded American people emerge from behind the subtle barriers erected to simulate the "security" our forefathers fled, or were torn from, we will be free. Until then we will continue to prosper materially. We will illuminate the universe with our collective genius. We will awe mankind. But we will not have proven that men of different backgrounds and races can live together serenely and pursue with shared enthusiasm understandings and undertakings that are closer, yet dimmer, than Mars. We will not, in short, have shown ourselves or others that Americanization is equivalent to humanization.

It is not enough to encourage egalitarianism with respect to today's American values. Michael Harrington, Kenneth Galbraith, and most recent Presidents have focused ample concern on the gap between the affluent society and the "other" America. But this has been in terms of assumed values that may in fact not be worth maintaining, never mind sharing. We must be willing to admit the possibility of even higher values, and someday speculate on what they might be, how to identify them, and how to share them.

In a Harper's (September 1969) magazine article, "In Russia," Arthur Miller writes, "At present, we are much more interested in what a thing is, how it works [than] in what it means." This judgment is very close to that of George Santayana, the native Spaniard who came to teach and love us and who wrote of Americans in *The Last Puritan*, "they respect only what you do, never what you think."

In *Character and Opinion in the United States*, Santayana wrote of "the pioneer,"

... he must work for the future, and it is healthy and dutiful of him to love his work for its own sake. At the same time unless reference to an ultimate purpose is at least virtual in all his activities, he runs the danger of becoming a living automaton, vain and ignominious in its mechanical constancy. Idealism about work can hide an internal materialism about life.

Latin American writers and philosophers have echoed this Spanish view of the Anglo-Colossus to the north. What is disturbing to some, but encouraging to others, is that young North Americans are beginning to voice the same concern. They do so as if they were the first to perceive it, which is a good thing. It proves that their own cultural legacies are not fashioned to stifle new growth. Most adult Americans don't share the same urge to know *why*. Knowing *that*, and knowing *how* are enough. Black America wants to know *if*, and also *when*. The answers to these latter questions lie deep in the American sub-conscious. The reflex responses of the conscious (and self-conscious) spokesmen of every viewpoint are guesses at best, the surface manifestations of a whole country turning something over in its mind. Meanwhile seeing ourselves as others see us—however distorted the image may appear—could give us perspectives to unlock a half century or more of captive emotions, and bring unimagined richness to our life.

The new world still remains undiscovered by us. The other Americas to the south of us with all their poverty and pain have something useful to tell us about our power and purpose. If we could but learn, as well as teach, the Americas would yield new gold to the exploring spirit of man. Meanwhile, if it is difficult to have great things expected of us and ironic to be held to standards few friends or adversaries can meet, we should remember that our challenge from the beginning has been to be the high standard bearer. We have proven the power of a diverse people to achieve order and prosperity in a new environment. The test we have yet to meet, and which a jealous yet hopeful world awaits, is not merely whether our institutions are sufficiently resilient to absorb our deepest aspirations, but whether we are. Our institutions —legal, economic, political, and educational—will survive and prosper if those who guide them and those who depend on them share a new awareness of the truly valuable things in human life, and look upon their pursuit as an exciting adventure. We should look on every fellow-citizen as indispensable to our quest, as if he were a signatory to a kind of Mayflower Compact for the next crossing. We and the world have cities to purify, schools and homes to build, fears to diminish, resources to conserve. But both our determination and our ability to achieve these goals will depend increasingly on a livelier and, if you will, more romantic appreciation of what it means to be men. Are the pragmatic men of the technological West incapable of this kind of awareness?

In *Technological Man*, Professor Victor Ferkiss of Georgetown University, writing of his first encounter with an astronaut, finds this "new man" a supertechnician, personable and exact, but ill at ease with emotion, beauty, and wonder. He generalizes from this one encounter to depict the astronauts as "the culmination of a long process of social development . . . technological man, come of age." Chet Huntley, formerly of NBC, calls them "dull." Generalizations of this kind are always tempting when they fit a preconception. But human nature, even in America, is full of surprises. And the untold disciplines that govern the life and work even of astronauts seem, in fact, not to have automated their reactions, much less "programed" their dreams. At least two of them have been dreaming of Congress, an unlikely orbit for the purely technological man.

A joint session of Congress was, in fact, privileged to hear Frank Borman's description of earth as seen from the moon—a tiny ball hanging in the black stillness of space. Borman said it brought home to him and his crewmen the true loneliness of mankind in the void of space. No solicitude for earth was noticeable in the galaxies. What help there might be for mankind must come, with

God's grace, from men. Thus, it was high time, they thought, to confirm earth's good in brotherhood.

Frank Borman, Neil Armstrong, and their crews were trained to move spacecraft, not hearts. But we were moved by the heartfelt words of a "personable young man" who, as Ferkiss writes, "in appearance and manner could just as well have been a rising junior executive in any large American corporation." Precisely. Doers can dream too, even the healthy and skilled. Those who merely analyze should not forbear from conversing with those who build. They might find they share the same dream. One dream of man is the increasing fulfillment of his best nature. The North American man concerns himself with it with growing interest and occasional fervor as his technological conquest of one kind of unknown brings him to the brink of another. He has talked about the dream before, but with too uncritical confidence in his assumptions—and generally at election time.

With every impending change in political fortunes and the onset of new administrations in American government, one is solemnly told to consider that he and his city, state, or country are at the threshold of a new day; that the opportunities outweigh the problems; and that the way to meet them is to vote for the man doing the talking. One has dutifully engaged in the discussion at four-year intervals at least. Now he has come to wonder what can be further meant by "new" days, deals, frontiers. What's on the other side from where we are? What do we want that we lack? What would a promised land offer? Peace, prosperity, jobs, perhaps, but even these we have to a large degree, as civilizations are measured. What would be really new for us, what no President can promise or provide, is an understanding of ourselves, and a decent respect for mankind, not just its opinions. That is the new dream.

Would high employment without inflation, booming trade, supersonic travel, elimination of the draft, riotless campuses, and a warless world help us to realize it? Would we then *know* our neighbors? Ironically, it has been *conflict*, in which we are joined against a common threat or pitted against one another, that has tended to bring such knowledge in the past. We have yet to perfect a social, much less a moral, equivalent of war. We have yet to learn how to make peace heroic. But desperate people communicate quite well. Between such "meetings" and total detachment there are mere encounters, which are mistaken for meetings.

PART ONE

UNDER THE RED CARPET

CHAPTER ONE

In 1957, a number of Welsh miners had gathered by the pit for a rare visit by his Excellency John Hay Whitney, the American ambassador to Great Britain. "How many of you," he asked cheerfully, "have ever met an ambassador from my country before?"

A hand went up in the back, an old man. "I did, sir."

"Tell us about it," said the Ambassador.

"I had the honor, sir, of escorting the body of one of your predecessors to the boat train." A courteous man, the old miner clearly considered this a second meeting, if not a second coming.

The incident illustrates with some exaggeration how the difference between a meeting and a mere encounter can be obscured by the human tendency to read more into the latter than circumstances justify. A schoolgirl's hand is pressed by a laughing candidate who is looking the other way. She squeals and tells her friends how she "met" the man.

Our lives are full of encounters in which the nonmeetings outnumber the meetings. "Confrontation," which denotes separation, even hostility, achieves acceptance as a synonym for "meeting," so alien to one another we become. Americans, particularly, are rather more "hail fellows" than well met. We hide from others and from ourselves behind the "good fences" that make us "good neighbors." We tend to measure the success of an encounter with another person by what we "get" out of it—the ticket, the admission, the job, the sale, the election. We spit out the seeds of one encounter, and go on to the next. How many people do we reflect on, and deeply admire? Those are the few we've *met*, and not many more. We are better trained and motivated to use people than to know them. Jet travel only multiplies the failures.

We should be grateful to humorists who, like fainting canaries in a coal mine, are often the first to identify the danger, in this case the pitfalls of normality. One of them has given us the story of an airline pilot's message to his passengers. "Folks, I've got two pieces of news for you—some good news and some bad news. I'll give you the bad news first: we're lost. Now the good news: we're traveling at record speed."

Honest conversation is the stabilizer of moving societies, without it they drift. Nor can it be abandoned to the media. It belongs to us all, without cosmetics, commercials, coaching, or clock watching—except for the Big Clock that ticks off man's chances to find an alternative to war. Most of us glance at it now and then. I do now as I reflect on the last eighteen years of my life in law, in public service, and on the political campaign trail.

My first election to Congress gave rise to feelings of satisfaction, subdued by the reminder that over one hundred thousand people voted against me. I thought of them, standing twelve yards apart on the road all the way from St. Louis to Washington, saying, "No!" It might be comforting in this case to believe, in spite of all the coffees, picnics, and factory and shopping center visits, we had not yet really "met." If we had, the significance was even less reassuring. But the assumption that voters would support an individual "if they only knew him" is one his family may make, but he had better not. He can be true to himself and therefore false to no other and still get whipped. That's what he will realize if his "self" is a demanding companion. To persuade others to accept that self, or even the shell that encases it, is a problem for politicians, people, and nations. What we so frequently forget is that the "others" whose understanding we seek, seek ours as well. Mutual understanding is really an exchange of gifts.

President Gustavo Díaz Ordaz, quoting Mexico's great Benito Juárez, reminded us in an address to Congress in 1967 that "respect for the rights of others is peace." It's a good place to begin. It always was. However, civilization's grim array of armies, mobs, kings, and priests have tended to demand respect from—not *for*—others, and since peace is built on minimal fulfillment of certain human requirements—dignity, decency—wars continue. Men yearn for peace, but they fight for dignity. Most thoughtful persons put a price on their dignity that mere power cannot meet. The price won't come down when it is high, and it will rise if it is low. To meet it is difficult today for commoner and king alike because each must surmount barriers of thoughtless custom. To take these down gently, lest they be brought down on our heads, is the task of the so-called *now* generation.

On a trip to Russia twelve years ago, I was asked again and again, *Kak vash zhisn?* "How is your life?" To know, or at least to care, what a man thinks of his own life, of the lives of others of the world, is to begin to "meet" him. What per cent of the people we "know," have we met in this way? Jean Jacques Rousseau once speculated on what the average person would do if, by a mere act of the will, "without leaving Paris," without discovery, and at great profit to himself, he could end the life of an old mandarin in Peking. Rousseau did not hold out much hope for the old mandarin. Thus, *tuer son mandarin*, "to kill his mandarin," became a modish expression for man's casual inhumanity to man. The crux was that the disposable man be remote. Sharon Tate and her friends were essentially strangers to their cult killers. The families at Mylai were said to be "not really people" to an overtaxed platoon. The disclosures of both tragedies broke the same week. History has a wry way of inviting comparisons. In one soul-searching week we were forced to consider two sets of victims of a kind of group hypnosis. We were inescapably called upon to question whether certain stresses could not produce identical behavior by the very types of Americans who are assumed to represent diametric opposites: the drug-culture hippie and the young soldier.

In his "Thoughts for The Times on War and Death," Freud contrasts the joyful return of World War I veterans with the need for atonement a savage warrior experienced. "He may not set foot in his village nor touch his wife until he has atoned for the murders committed in war by penances . . . a vein of ethical sensitiveness which has been lost by us civilized men." This must have been before the scalp, the niche on the pistol grip, and the coonskin on the wall. And, as John Nef points out in his *War and Human Progress*, "by 1914 the Western mind encouraged war by making a spiritual value out of organized fighting."

Loss of this "ethical sensitiveness," conscience, like loss of memory, is unaccountable, but quite predictable in the collective mesmerisms of our time—war, race hatred, drugs. Each evokes and tends to justify the kind of impersonal cruelty that society, shorn of its adherence to the First Commandment, or the primeval taboo it expresses, seeks yet to punish. The impersonal kind of assault and homicide, which has claimed the lives of so many innocent passersby, store clerks, and filling station attendants, is not looked on with horror. In America our record of traffic fatalities, running at 50,000 per year, bespeaks a high collective threshold of tolerance for incidental genocide via the iron guarantor of our continued mutual alienation, the automobile, which kills quickly while its exhaust kills slowly. Televised bloodshed in the name of entertainment does not teach badly, it reflects dispassionately what we have already been badly taught.

Our recent demands for "law and order" and clean air and water prove our capacity for indignation. But indignation is not remorse. Many of the world's youth sense that the price of their "civilization" is lost remorse. To the society that acknowledges the Commandment, "Thou shalt not kill," those who say, "I don't want to," should be the object of understanding concern, not of scorn. Nor should their sincerity be measured by some prolonged exposure to a "system of belief." The gold of love is where we find it. That one belief alone, naked, inexplicable, and defiant, may do more to save civilization than the pedantry of a thousand scholars.

What opportunity for remorse regained is there now in the nuclear age which gives unprecedented scope for callousness? To dispatch a hundred million "Red" Chinese with a few fireballs would be considered a normal security measure by some today. If there are others who fervently work to preserve their fellow-man, they are a nucleus only. Concern has its thousands; apathy its ten thousands. An ironic corollary to Rousseau's theory is the number of those who would spend money and concern to revive an old mandarin, but not a needy family downtown. Charity that begins away from home doesn't bring the donor into embarrassing contact or an evolving relationship with the beneficiary. We've learned to endure the suffering of others nearer at hand. We prefer to give without meeting. Men who have been at the receiving end of such gifts will tell you that such giving is more like taking.

Obviously, giving doesn't appear selfless unless some self is given. Mere noblesse doesn't oblige; sensitivity and honest interest, must be included along with what Ben Franklin called "a doubt of our own infallability." What Lincoln called the "better angels of our nature" need exercise. They have sat with folded wings in the recesses of our national conscience while defective communication and disparate power made our world safe for complacency.

In the past it was relaxing to sense how much time had to elapse between a social explosion in some other corner of the world and its sound in ours. At times it never reached us. But radio and television have shunted the gap between the lightning and thunder. Today every home records the tremors. What is our response? We react by calling on "wise leadership" to bring us through. What about our leadership? Is it to be wise while we are foolish, patient while we fume, creative while we destroy? Occasionally, as the publicists of competing nations are routinely sticking pins in one another's images, their leaders meet to pull them out. What can be accomplished at a summit with so much confusion at the base? It is a question put in part to protocol.

The principal function of official protocol is to establish

and maintain the context in which meetings between government leaders can occur with a minimum of misunderstanding. I do not say a maximum of comfort for there is nothing comfortable about the tortuous rituals to which world leaders are led to submit by "tradition."

Guidelines become straitjackets. But official protocol, even dragging the chains of custom, is creative work. No visit is a perfect format for the next. No two meetings are alike. We try to achieve the projection of a unified national purpose with respect to the vital questions of our time. But no nation can project what it does not have, and until we have met one another at home, we' cannot, nor can anyone on our behalf, present a credible front to others. We can "prepare a face to meet a face," and a "table in the presence." So men have done for thousands of wartorn years. If man would do more, what resources could he call upon? Commonality of language, age, culture—none of these is guaranteed to turn an encounter into a meeting. Mechanical transmission, instant replay, and jet travel are as likely to prove impediments as assets to the conversation. Nor are death or separation necessary bars to it. The sensitive man, the listening man, is the peace builder. Those long gone whom we know only by their work or art or music or thought, we can know well enough to be enriched, to understand, to follow, or to avoid. What we must do is devote the same care, the same passion, the same diligence to understanding the living, however unaccomplished. And, above all, the same sense of humor.

It is all but impossible to change something you have never laughed at. Men sense that there is something laughable in pomp and ceremony, because it usually involves a certain conscious pretense. We want to laugh sometimes but we hold ourselves in check to spare feelings or avoid censure. Our restraint is eventually misinterpreted as respect. As chief of protocol I was given some new reassurance almost every day that absurdity reigned in high places. My tenure began with a message from my neighbor, Art Buchwald, who, noting my appointment, concluded morosely that "the neighborhood is going all to hell." Other irreverent messages arrived including a telegram with the reminder, "It don't mean a thing if you ain't got that king."

CHAPTER TWO

Speaking before the Women's Press Corps after some months in office, I told the ladies I was doing everything by the book, the book being *Around the World Backwards and Sideways* by Robert Benchley. *My Ten Years In a Quandary*, another Benchley immortal, would also have qualified. My two years as chief of protocol were, in fact, on one level, a bewildering array of culs de sac, unmusical chairs, people where spaces should be and spaces where people belonged, albeit sustained by a gritty staff and a vague awareness that this, too, would pass.

The assignment began—like so many things began and ended in those days—suddenly. On the 18th of March, 1966, as director of the President's Committee on Juvenile Delinquency, I was attending a Columbia Law School Board of Visitors meeting, taking a back seat to eminent lawyers, jurists, and professors who remembered my academic record well enough not to expect anything startling from me. We were discussing the "relevance" of the law school curriculum when I was called to the telephone. Even as I picked it up I heard a familiar Texas voice stating that Ambassador Lloyd Hand had resigned as chief of protocol, and asking me to replace him. "Will you do it?" the voice asked.

"Yes, sir, Mr. President" was the best I could come up
with on such short notice. By the time I had called my
wife, reporters and photographers were already closing
in on our home. The announcement must have been
made instantly. I asked my wife to answer all their questions very effectively, while I went ahead with a dinner
engagement with old friends in New York. It was the last
night of comfortable anonymity for a long time.

Two days later I received the oath under the avuncular
gaze of Secretary Dean Rusk who announced to those
assembled that I had "graduated from the world of
juvenile delinquency into the world of adult delinquency." My deputy, Chester Carter, then handed me a
couple of oversized envelopes and pushed me through the
crowd down to a waiting limousine. There were only
minutes to go before the arrival at the White House of
the ambassador from the Sudan whom I was to present to
the President. "Mr. President, this is the Ambassador.
Ambassador, this is the President," I mumbled in the car.
Mr. Carter corrected this simplified version to "Mr. President—his Excellency the Ambassador of Sudan," then
dropped me off at the Diplomatic entrance to the White
House, and wished me well.

I introduced myself to the officers of the honor guard,
surveyed the beauty of the South Lawn and waited with
confidence for the ambassador's limousine. It swung into
view, flags flying. The guardsmen lining the drive
snapped to present arms as it passed. When it pulled up
I was courteously headed off by an officer who opened
the door. A substantial gentleman emerged in morning
suit with sash and ribbons. He spoke French which was
reasonable for a Sudanese, and I responded more or less
in the same language. I had some questions for his riding

escort, an assistant chief of protocol, but he waved cordially, and the car drove off.

I escorted the ambassador through the Diplomatic entrance into the lower lobby of the White House. The guards and ushers smiled. Here was the chief of protocol with an ambassador to present—make way for the chief. The question in my mind was which way precisely to go. I had not navigated this part of the White House before. I looked at the ushers with an expression that should have conveyed a sincere interest in being helped. They smiled and backed away. Here comes the chief. Thus abandoned, I considered my options. But it was not a time for indecision. I swung my charge smartly up to a likely looking door, opened it, and we found ourselves in a coat closet, with brooms besides, and other domestic paraphernalia. I looked up at the ambassador to see how he was getting on. He was fine. He said it was his first time in the United States, as if to indicate he was unfamiliar with this part of the ritual. I told him it was my first day on the job. "Now, let's go find the President." The ushers took a keener interest in us. We made it to the Treaty Room in the family quarters where the ambassador signed "the book," and to the Yellow Oval Room where the presentation was made flawlessly—except for some indecision on my part as to which envelopes to retain, which relinquish, and which drop on the floor. Sudan did not break relations with us until the following year, and this was due, I feel certain, not so much to this incident as to the international repercussions of the Six-Day War.

The ladies of the press were present at every such presentation, standing primly to one side and scratching on their little pads. I was to learn their power. No matter

what has actually happened, history probably will be
known as they have written it. I also learned something
about the relative importance of chiefs of protocol on
these occasions. As I positioned myself for my first event,
a photographer's voice rang out, "Hey, Jim, outta the
way!" Another yelped, "This way, over there; that's it;
stay there!" Other friendly instructions were given by the
photographic corps ranging from the agile and lightly-
armed acrobatic types to the perspiring native bearers of
the heavy equipment, shoulders sagging and knees
buckling under their burdens. The chief of protocol's
dignity today is not nearly as important as tomorrow's
pictures.

If I didn't stand on my dignity, it was because I knew
it wouldn't hold me up. My job was to stay on my toes
and off other people's. Once when the Marine band struck
up "Hail to the Chief," I turned to the President and said,
"Our song." His expression indicated that, whether he
heard it or not, it did not bear repeating.

Unfamiliar surroundings accounted for another entrap-
ment. Hassan II, King of Morocco, had elected to arrive
for his state visit aboard the Italian luxury liner, SS *Raffaello*. With his Majesty and over 150 retainers the ship
moved gracefully into New York harbor on the freezing
8th of February, 1967. My wife and I, together with Bud
Palmer (Mayor John Lindsay's director of public events),
Mrs. Palmer, and the Moroccan ambassador, rode a Navy
cutter out to the *Raffaello*. We went aboard and waited
on his Majesty. The King amiably greeted us and
remained with us until we docked at the pier. Since
authority and responsibility for the arrangements to
debark were more or less evenly divided between the
State Department, Security, the Navy, Customs officials,

and the New York police, no plan had been devised, and it was every King for himself. Photographers, passengers, sightseers, longshoremen, and police surged around us in an amorphous mass as I led the King and his two small children from ship to shore. Helpless security officers, with their static-filled walkie-talkies held aloft, tried to give aid and comfort to our little band. Followed closely by the King in his fitted overcoat, I walked briskly toward a tall and apparently commanding police officer. He was tall, but commanded nothing save the small space he was standing on next to a doorless wall. The cameras and the curious closed in. Within less than a minute we would have been part of the crowd itself and no longer the sympathetic object of its interest. Its interest would then have been like ours, to find an escape from the crush. I found myself shouting, "Back, back, we're coming through!" and making slicing motions with my arm. It had a marvelous effect. People did make way, and we soon found ourselves in the carpeted quiet of the Mayor's limousine. How or if all those other people ever disentangled themselves, I cannot say. His Majesty then placed a call to Mayor Lindsay on the radio-telephone. They laughed a great deal.

On other occasions unmanageable crowds removed from Protocol the scheduling of moves of the official party. One was President Johnson's arrival in Mexico City, April, 1967. This was a hastily arranged visit. Originally, only Mrs. Johnson was to make the trip. The first inkling I had that the President himself might go was the delivery of twenty gray flannel serapes to the Secret Service. At least that is what I told inquiring reporters. The main event was to be the unveiling of Felix de Welden's graceful statue of Lincoln in a Mexico City park. I was given

about thirty hours' notice, and dispatched my deputy,
Chester Carter, to prepare the scenario. He did a masterly
job, but it was a little hard to absorb in three minutes as I
emerged from *Air Force I* with the President and his party
to the resoundingly off-key welcome of an assortment of
bands. The Mexican chief of protocol was an experienced
man, but I could see by his stricken countenance and
vague arm-flappings that he had had as little chance to
prepare for the visit as I. Somehow the two Presidents
were herded to the rostrum and delivered their respective
remarks. It was on the drive to the President's palace
that bedlam broke. At least one million Mexicans lined
the drive, which was estimated to take thirty minutes. It
took three hours. The two Presidents were not mindful
of scheduling problems as they beamed, waved, and shook
hands from their open car. I was farther back in line with
the genial and accomplished Mexican ambassador to the
United States, Hugo Margain. Frequently, citizens would
lean into the window and shout, "Merry Christmas!" an
expression of friendship on that April day. Many recognized the Ambassador and yelled, "Hi, Hugo!" I wondered
what American ambassador would be recognized in his
own capital. When we arrived at the palace, pandemonium
swirled about the doors. I was swept in, and once inside
asked for Secretary Rusk. "My God," said a security man,
"he's still out there!" We opened the door a crack and
there was the imperturbable countenance of Dean Rusk,
bobbing placidly in a sea of tossing sombreros.

I was excluded from the informal dinner which followed and during which the President, in spite of mutual
protocol pledges to avoid gift-giving, was given a gift. I
had not been prepared for such friendly deception, but
the President's reaction convinced me of the value of such

preparedness in the future. I had certainly let my President down. I had done so by taking at face value the assertion of a Latin American that *his* President would not succumb to impulse. The assurance was formalistic, the gesture was human, and I learned that one simply can't trust a Latin not to be generous.

An unexpected dimension to the job unfolded at the dedication next day when the President, disturbed by the noisy rotors of a low-flying helicopter, told me to "get it out of there." After transmitting this order to security personnel, and observing some of the greatest shrugs in the West, I stared at the helicopter very disapprovingly myself. After a few moments it veered away, and the President nodded his satisfaction. I had heard of "talking down" stricken aircraft. The challenge here was "thinking down" a serviceable one.

The Mexican crowds were huge, but the biggest crowd I ever expect to see was gathered in Seoul, Korea, to greet the President in October, 1966. From the raised dais it was possible to see nearly a million people, and to believe that the streets radiating from the square harbored thousands more, concealed from us by buildings, but converging desperately for a closer look. At times portions of the crowd swayed dangerously. Riot police trained to anticipate and deal with this phenomenon would run in a wedge formation directly into such groups, swinging their clubs briskly and with authority. It had a stabilizing effect. People righted themselves and calmed down. When the speeches were over, the relative importance of protocol officials was brought home to me with a kind of genial finality. With security officers and Korean guards, I assisted the Presidential party to their waiting limousines. Other dignitaries boarded theirs. My car was down

the line but, as I finally made my way to it, the joyous
crowd broke the police lines and exploded into the avenue. The motorcade started up and kept moving. Standard procedure in these cases is to keep going. To stop
means to allow pedestrians to get between the cars, and
that, in countries where human life is valued, spells the
end to order and progress. My own car was gathering
speed in stately fashion a good forty yards from me. Nor
was it possible to board it on the run, as I had so often
done in Australia during the President's awesome campaign of that Texas-like land. It was a question of not
letting the cars out of sight. It was my first day in Seoul,
and I didn't know my way around too well. I broke into
a trot, surrounded by boy scouts, schoolgirls, shopkeep-
ers, soldiers, and police. Together we all ran after the
long black line of limousines, which disappeared slowly
around the bend. I was in pretty good shape for a chief
of protocol, and kept pace with the front runners, finally
overtaking a car that had been separated from the pack.
A familiar face leaned out, with the trace of a smile.
"Would you like a ride?"

"Yes, thank you, Mr. Secretary," I replied, and climbed
into the Rusk limousine. I wasn't too worried. Had I
been outdistanced, the friendly crowd would have fed
and watered me until help arrived.

Motorcades I have mourned include one carrying
President Hamani Diori of Niger from Blair House to the
airport. I interrupted it myself. Under general protocol
instructions, the principal departs on time if he is ready
and willing. The presence of the chief of protocol is
highly desirable but not essential. I was caught in traffic
two blocks from Blair House. The red lights on the squad
cars began spinning. The motorcycles swung out onto

Pennsylvania Avenue. The great Lincoln cast off from its
mooring and glided swiftly. I leapt from my trapped car,
sprinted and jumped into the limousine as it turned down
17th Street. President Diori seemed gratified to see me,
and our security officers were kind enough to recognize
me in time. It was on just such a whirlwind spin to the
airport that King Constantine II of Greece turned to me
and said, "Where are we headed now?"

"The airport, your Majesty."

"Not at all," he replied; "I have another appointment
with the President."

We radioed the escort and the parade of cars ground
to a halt. With my charge looking on, bemused, I called
the White House, not, of course, to confirm the King's
recollection, but to ascertain if the President was "ready."
He was. The two Chiefs of State had merely neglected
to tell anyone else of their decision. But ignorance is no
defense in protocol where clairvoyance is nine-tenths of
the law.

There are times when a young protocol chief's fancy
turns to security, sometimes synonymous with comfort but
not always. The dead end on the pier during King
Hassan's arrival and various motorcade happenings made
me keenly aware of the fateful combinations of circumstance, the anticipation of which had long since lined the
stern faces of veteran security officers. The unplanned
foray into surprised throngs may be the safest for the
principals in contrast to scheduled stops that alert "those
who plan some evil," as the hymn goes. In either case we
learn that security, like diplomacy itself, is everybody's
business.

One welcoming throng that nearly killed with kind-
ness was outside the Lennon Hotel in Sydney, Australia,

on the Asian trip. After the President had entered the hotel, the entrance was blocked with happy well-wishers, some holding up children and, in one or two cases, their dogs, for a better look. One told me, "If it hadn't been for you Yanks, I'd be pushing a rickshaw in these streets." Then more came—from all directions—with no outlet but the blocked hotel doorway. Women screamed, men fell. Two children separated from their mother, held hands, wide-eyed beside me. Suddenly they were pushed flat to the street. I picked them up and planted them on top of my limousine. This started a kind of bucket brigade. The very young and the faint or feeble were handed over the heads of the crowd to high ground, the car tops, where they sat with their feet dangling over the sides until troopers finally cleared the area. All in a day's work.

Security officers generally don't rough up the dignitary they are assigned to protect. But this isn't always the case. They may do so in the line of duty to avoid a worse fate. Thus at the conclusion of the mass celebrating President Joaquin Balaguer's inauguration in the Dominican Republic, Vice President Hubert Humphrey was virtually given a "bum's rush" out of the cathedral of Santo Domingo located in the heart of the leftist leader Francisco Caamaño's territory. Smiling gamely he was tossed like a sack of meal into the waiting convertible. With colleagues all but sitting on the genial Vice President as he tried feebly to free a hand to wave, two secret service men, perched on the seatbacks with shotguns, peered attentively at the admiring crowd. The convertible drove off like a bee-stung filly to top off this solemn ceremony.

Security was only slightly less gentle with Prime Minister Harold Wilson as he left Blair House one afternoon to see the President. A man with a rifle had been reported entering a building diagonally across the street. The Prime Minister, not fazed in the least, skipped smartly into the car a step ahead of the friendly push he would otherwise have been dealt.

Many of the world's guest houses are remote, inaccessible, and heavily guarded mansions or palaces. Blair House, as the Puerto Rican terrorists who assaulted it to get to President Truman learned, is just a house across the street from the White House, and a bus stop where people might be waiting in line for a bus, and might not. Making a slow U-turn there with the Shah of Iran, our limousine was rushed by dissident Iranian students who were waiting in fact for *our* bus. They hurled petitions against the windows, fortunately nothing harder. But the opportunity was there. Protocol often defers reluctantly to the discomforts of Security, but this occasion prompted me to inquire of Security if it had ever considered housing presidential guests in a more secluded area. I was told the problem had been under study for some time. It is true, as President Kennedy once prophetically observed, that total protection from a mad man's intent is illusory. But if the decision to abandon Blair House as the official guest residence is ever made, I hope it is made before, not after, a tragic fact of this kind. To date, the dominant hazards that test the endurance of state visitors are in ceremony, not in security. And the ceremonial hazards also invite review and reform.

CHAPTER THREE

The highest category of visit to a nation by the head of state of another nation is denominated a state visit. An "official" visit in United States protocol parlance is a visit by a head of government as distinct from a chief of state. Britain's prime minister, for example, is her head of Government; the Queen, her Chief of State. Our President is both and could be received in either capacity.

In the United States, either type of visit generally involves two or more months of planning, two and a half days in Washington and six touring the country. For this period, lodgings, travel, and entertainment are provided the visitor and his official party (maximum twelve persons, plus incidental personal staff, valets, etc.) at United States expense. Normally the visitor is expected to leave the country following the official period, but naturally he is not required to do so. He is, however, virtually required to leave the capital, and any departure from normal practice should be handled very discreetly so as not to set difficult precedents. A certain state visitor to France, for example, with the intention of remaining for a private visit, boarded the departing plane from Paris waving to the cheering throng. The plane taxied a brief distance down the runway, stopped, and the visitor stepped out.

The pilot had been instructed to fly to another field but got confused. In a more organized way the King of Nepal, during his visit to the United States, carried out an old wish to hunt bear in Alaska following completion of the official portion of his visit in 1967. But it is the official part of this visit that I believe may serve to illustrate the planning involved.

The visit itself was conceived and implemented in the context of the geographical position of this small, landlocked country of ten million persons, wedged between two major powers engaged in a continuing pattern of tension and conflict. Nepal, anxious to maintain correct and, if possible, cordial relations with both, follows a generally nonaligned policy. It had been promised considerable Chinese Communist aid, but a road from Kathmandu, its capital, to the Tibetan border was about all that had been realized. Moreover, it did not go unnoticed that it would well serve the Chinese themselves in the event they wished to proceed to newly annexed territory in that fashion.

Nepal's cultural, religious, and linguistic ties are much closer to India, which, in view of Nepal's strategic location in the Himalayan defense perimeter, has asserted it will not countenance encroachments on its territorial integrity. India also provides considerable aid in the form of health, hydroelectric, and industrial projects. Nepal and the United Kingdom have had varying relationships for a century and a half, and the famed Gurkha troops serving with the British Army are Nepalese nationals. The Soviet Union opened an embassy in 1959, and has also offered economic aid, including another road. State visits were exchanged in 1958 and 1960 with the Soviet Union, and with Britain in 1960 and 1961. Our own policy had emphasized economic aid, over $100 million since formal relations were established in 1947, and running about $10 million annually, for education, rural development, communications, forestry, small industry, and the development of local government institutions. We had given limited arms assistance to the Royal Nepalese Army, but deferred largely to India and the United Kingdom in that regard. Our policy objectives included: support for Nepalese independence and territorial integrity; support for the Nepalese effort to develop human and social resources through economic aid and technical assistance; and support for increased participation in Nepalese development by other free world countries. It was in the light of the forgoing factors that the state visit of his Majesty Mahendra Bir Bikram Shah Deva, King of Nepal, and her Majesty Ratna Rajya Lakshmi Devi Shah, Queen of Nepal, to the United States occurred in the fall of 1967. The following extracts from the Office of Protocol's administrative arrangements for the visit give an insight into some of the detail involved.

We pick up the schedule Monday, October 30, 1967:

DEPARTMENT OF STATE
Washington, D. C.
OFFICE OF THE CHIEF OF PROTOCOL

VISIT TO THE UNITED STATES OF AMERICA OF THEIR MAJESTIES
THE KING AND QUEEN OF NEPAL

Administrative Arrangements
for the Departure from Washington, D. C.
of the Chief of Protocol
and the Arrival at John F. Kennedy International Airport of
Their Majesties the King and Queen of Nepal

Monday, October 30, 1967

At 4:00 P.M. EST, the United States Air Force special
flight will depart from Andrews Air Force Base for John F.
Kennedy International Airport, New York. The flying time
is 50 minutes and we are scheduled to arrive in New York
at 4:50 P.M. EST.

Arrangements have been made with Air France to use the
Air France reception area to wait for the arrival of Their
Majesties.

Their Majesties are scheduled to arrive at John F. Kennedy
International Airport at 7:00 P.M. EST aboard Air France
flight #17. His Royal Highness, Ambassador and Mrs. Khatri
and Ambassador and Mrs. Symington will proceed from the
reception room at 6:50 P.M. to the gate of arrival of Air
France flight #17.

The remaining members of the Welcoming Committee
should await the arrival of Their Majesties at the Air France
reception room.

Ambassador Khatri and Ambassador Symington will board
the aircraft to greet Their Majesties upon its arrival. They
will then escort Their Majesties to the Welcoming Committee
assembled in the reception room.

During the welcoming the baggage will be transferred from
the Air France aircraft to the United States Air Force special
aircraft.

At 7:30 P.M., Ambassador and Mrs. Symington will escort
Their Majesties to the United States Air Force special flight.

At 7:40 P.M., Their Majesties and their party will depart
from New York City aboard a United States Air Force special
flight for Langley Air Force Base, Virginia.

DEPARTMENT OF STATE
Washington, D. C.
OFFICE OF THE CHIEF OF PROTOCOL

VISIT TO THE UNITED STATES OF AMERICA OF THEIR MAJESTIES
THE KING AND QUEEN OF NEPAL

Administrative Arrangements for the Arrival at
Langley Air Force Base and Williamsburg, Virginia

Monday, October 30, 1967

Their Majesties the King and Queen of Nepal and their party will arrive at Langley Air Force Base, Virginia, aboard a United States Air Force special flight at 8:40 P.M. EST, on Monday, October 30, 1967.

Members of the Nepalese Party Aboard the Aircraft
(See Enclosure Number One)

Upon arrival of the aircraft, protocol, security, and press staff will leave the aircraft to insure that proper arrangements have been made on the ground.

Members of the Official Nepalese and American parties should leave the aircraft in order of precedence. Ambassador Symington will present the Welcoming Committee to Their Majesties.

Upon completion of the greetings, Ambassador and Mrs. Symington will escort Their Majesties to the waiting helicopter.

At 8:50 P.M., the party will depart from Langley Air Force Base, Virginia, and proceed to Williamsburg, Virginia.

At 9:05 P.M., Their Majesties and their party will arrive at Williamsburg, Virginia.

Ambassador Symington will present the members of the Welcoming Committee to Their Majesties.

Upon completion of the greetings, Their Majesties will depart the landing site for the Allen Byrd House. Other members of the party will be escorted to their residences.

ENCLOSURE NO. 1

His Majesty
  MAHENDRA Bir Bikram
    Shah Deva
    King of Nepal
Her Majesty
  RATNA Rajya Lakshmi
    Devi Shah
    Queen of Nepal
His Royal Highness
  BIRENDRA Bir Bikram
    Shah Deva
    Crown Prince of Nepal
His Excellency
  Kirti Nidhi BISTA
    Deputy Prime Minister
    and Foreign Minister of
    Nepal
Mrs. BISTA
His Excellency
  Major General Padma
    Bahadur KHATRI
    Ambassador of Nepal
    to the United States
Mrs. KHATRI
Major General
  Sher Bahadur MALLA
    Principal Military Secretary
    to His Majesty
Bada Kazi Pushpa
  Raj RAJBHANDARI
    Principal Personal Secre-
    tary to His Majesty
Mir Subba Ishwari Man
  SHRESTHA
    Secretary to His Majesty
Mir Subba
  Madhusudan Raj
    RAJBHANDARI
    Private Secretary
    to His Majesty

Mir Subba Renu Lal SINGH
  Press Secretary
    to His Majesty
His Excellency
  Yadu Nath KHANAL
    Foreign Secretary
Major General
  Shushil Chandra
    HALDER
    Personal Physician
    to His Majesty
Field Marshal
  Nir Shumshere Jung
    Bahadur RANA
    Former Commander-in-
    Chief, Nepalese Army
Major General
  Mohan Bikram SHAH
    Royal Treasurer
Colonel Shushil Shumshere
  Jung Bahadur RANA
    Queen's brother and
    Officer-in-Charge of the
    Royal Flight
Mr. Mahendra Nath
  KHANAL
    Director,
    Department of Culture
Mr. Badri Prasad KHANAL
  Section Officer,
    Ministry of External
    Affairs
Mr. Manindra Raj
  SHRESTHA
    Editor, Motherland,
    Nepalese Newspaper
Professor Narayan
  Prasad SHRESTHA
    Traveling Companion
    to the Crown Prince

DEPARTMENT OF STATE
Washington, D. C.
OFFICE OF THE CHIEF OF PROTOCOL

VISIT TO THE UNITED STATES OF AMERICA OF THEIR MAJESTIES
THE KING AND QUEEN OF NEPAL

Administrative Arrangements
for the Arrival at the White House

Wednesday, November 1, 1967

Their Majesties the King and Queen of Nepal and their party will arrive at President's Park (Ellipse) by helicopter at 11:25 A.M. EST from Williamsburg, Virginia. The party will proceed immediately by car to the South Lawn of the White House.

Welcoming Committee

Members of the Welcoming Committee are requested to arrive at the South Lawn of the White House by 11:10 A.M., entering the White House grounds at the Southwest Gate and proceeding to the Diplomatic Entrance.

Arrival Ceremonies

At 11:25 A.M., President and Mrs. Johnson will depart from the President's Office. The trumpets will play four ruffles and flourishes and "Hail to the Chief." During the playing of "Hail to the Chief," President and Mrs. Johnson will walk to the vicinity of the platform to await the arrival of Their Majesties the King and Queen of Nepal.

At 11:30 A.M., Their Majesties the King and Queen of Nepal accompanied by the Honorable James W. Symington, Chief of Protocol of the United States, and Mrs. Symington, will enter the Southwest Gate of the White House. The trumpets will sound a fanfare as the cars approach. The car carrying Their Majesties will stop at the Diplomatic Entrance

Continued

where Ambassador Symington will present Their Majesties to President and Mrs. Johnson. Then Secretary and Mrs. Rusk and Admiral and Mrs. Moorer will be introduced. While photographs are being taken of the greetings, protocol officers will assist the members of the Nepalese party to their places to the right of the platform.

Following the photographs, President and Mrs. Johnson will escort Their Majesties onto the platform. Others, as indicated below, will take their places on the platform.

PLATFORM

Her Majesty	President Johnson	His Majesty	Mrs. Johnson
Deputy Prime Minister Bista	Secretary Rusk		His Royal Highness
Ambassador Symington	Admiral Moorer	Ambassador Laise	Ambassador Khatri

When all are in position, the Commander of Troops will bring the Honor Guard to Present Arms.

As the Commander of Troops salutes, the trumpets will sound four ruffles and flourishes and the band will play the national anthem of Nepal, followed by the national anthem of the United States. A 21-gun salute will be fired simultaneously with the music.

Upon completion of honors, the troops will be given Order Arms, the Commander will salute and report, "Sir, the Honor Guard is formed."

President Johnson will escort His Majesty toward the band. The Commander of Troops will take a position to the right of His Majesty and guide him through the inspection. As the inspection party turns in front of the band, President Johnson will take a position to the right of the Commander of Troops.

The band will play appropriate music during the inspection. The inspection will begin at the right front of the band. The inspection party will pass along the front rank of troops. Members of the inspection party will render salutes when passing in front of the Colors. When the inspection party reaches the left flank of the Honor Guard, it will pass around the rear of the formation and around the band. When passing in rear of the Colors, salutes will not be rendered by members of the inspection party.

Continued

When the inspection party reaches the right front of the band, the Commander of Troops will halt, salute and report, "Sir, this completes the inspection." President Johnson will escort His Majesty back to the platform. The Commander of Troops will return to his post and bring the Honor Guard to Present Arms. He and his staff will salute His Majesty. After bringing the Honor Guard to Order Arms, the Commander will salute and report, "Sir, this concludes the ceremony."

The President and His Majesty will move to the microphone at the left side of the platform. President Johnson will welcome Their Majesties to the United States and His Majesty will respond.

Upon conclusion of the remarks, President and Mrs. Johnson will escort Their Majesties into the Diplomatic Reception Room. Secretary and Mrs. Rusk and Admiral and Mrs. Moorer will join them and a receiving line will be formed on the east side of the room.

Members of the official Nepalese party and the Welcoming Committee will be escorted into the Diplomatic Reception Room where they will be presented to President and Mrs. Johnson, Their Majesties the King and Queen of Nepal, Secretary and Mrs. Rusk, and Admiral and Mrs. Moorer. After each person has been presented, he will leave by the same door by which he entered.

President Johnson will escort His Majesty to the President's car on the driveway at the Diplomatic Entrance. Mrs. Johnson and Her Majesty will enter the First Lady's car which will be behind the President's car.

The motorcade will leave the White House grounds by the Southeast Gate and proceed by the following route: East on Hamilton Place, turning north on 14th Street, Southwest on New York Avenue to Pennsylvania Avenue, terminating at Blair House.

Upon arrival at Blair House, President and Mrs. Johnson will take their leave and return to the White House.

With the departure of President and Mrs. Johnson, the royal guests prepared for the Secretary of State's luncheon and the following rigorous schedule:

1:15 P.M.   The Secretary of State and Mrs. Rusk will give a luncheon in honor of Their Majesties in the Benjamin Franklin Room, Department of State.

3:00 P.M.   Departure from the Department of State.

3:05 P.M.   Arrival at Arlington National Cemetery, where His Majesty will place wreaths at the tomb of the Unknown Soldier and at the grave of the late President John F. Kennedy.

3:35 P.M.   Departure from Arlington National Cemetery and return to Blair House.

        4:30 P.M.   Her Majesty will visit the Children's Hospital, 2125 13th Street, N.W.

5:00 P.M.   His Majesty will meet with President Johnson at the White House.

8:00 P.M.   The President and Mrs. Johnson will give a dinner in honor of Their Majesties the King and Queen of Nepal at the White House. Dress: Black tie.

Thursday, November 2

10:00 A.M.   Secretary Rusk will meet with His Majesty at Blair House.

        10:00 A.M.   Her Majesty will visit the National Gallery of Art.

        11:00 A.M.   Departure from the National Gallery of Art.

        11:15 A.M.   Arrival at the National Geographic Society, 1145 17th Street, N.W. Her Majesty will visit the National Geographic Society.

Continued

12:00 noon   The National Press Club will give a luncheon in honor of His Majesty at the National Press Club Building, 14th and F Streets, N.W.

12:30 P.M.   Her Majesty will have lunch privately at Blair House.

3:00 P.M.   Her Majesty will visit Gallaudet College for the Deaf, 7th and Florida Avenue, N.W.

4:00 P.M.   The Honorable Stuart Symington, Chairman of the Senate Foreign Relations Subcommittee will give a coffee in honor of His Majesty at the Capitol, Room S116.

6:00 P.M.   Their Majesties the King and Queen of Nepal will receive Chiefs of the Diplomatic Missions and their wives at the International Ballroom, Washington Hilton Hotel.

6:30 P.M.   By command of Their Majesties the King and Queen of Nepal, His Excellency Kirti Nidhi Bista, Deputy Prime Minister of Nepal will give a reception in honor of President and Mrs. Johnson in the International Ballroom, Washington Hilton Hotel.

9:00 P.M.   Their Majesties will have dinner privately at the Embassy of Nepal, 2730 34th Place, N.W.

Friday, November 3

10:15. A.M.   Their Majesties and party will depart from the Blair House.

10:20 A.M.   Arrival at the Washington Monument Grounds where a military departure ceremony will be conducted. The Secretary of State will head the Farewell Committee.

Continued

10:35 A.M. EST	Departure from the Washington Monument Grounds by United States Marine Corps helicopter flight. (Flying time: 35 minutes)
11:10 A.M. EST	Arrival at the Eisenhower Farm, Gettysburg, Pennsylvania. Their Majesties will meet with former President Dwight D. Eisenhower.
11:50 A.M. EST	Departure from the Eisenhower Farm by United States Marine Corps helicopter flight. (Flying time: 35 minutes)
12:25 P.M. EST	Arrival at Andrews Air Force Base, Maryland.
12:35 P.M. EST	Departure from Andrews Air Force Base, Maryland, aboard a United States Air Force special flight. (Luncheon will be served aboard.) (Flying time: 2 hours)
2:35 P.M. EST	Arrival at the Skid Strip, John F. Kennedy Space Center, National Aeronautics and Space Administration, Florida. Their Majesties will tour the facilities of John F. Kennedy Space Center, NASA.
7:15 P.M. EST	Departure from the Skid Strip, John F. Kennedy Space Center, National Aeronautics Space Center, Florida. (Flight time: 2 hours and 20 minutes)
9:35 P.M. EST	Arrival at John F. Kennedy International Airport, New York.
9:50 P.M.	Departure from the airport.
10:20 P.M.	Arrival at the Waldorf Towers, where Their Majesties will reside during their stay in New York.

The remainder of the New York schedule included visits with leading American industrialists, with Mayor Lindsay, with John D. Rockefeller, head of the Asia Foundation, to the Lincoln Center, and to the United Nations where the King conferred with Secretary-General U Thant and addressed the General Assembly. Then he took his well-earned side trip to Alaskan bear country.

Exactly what reassurances either the King or we gained from this frenetic sojourn is not known. Clearly the overblown rhetoric of welcoming speeches and dinner toasts with their attestations of good will "in which all America joins" can mean little to a sensible person who realizes very few Americans even know he's here, and who places his sole reliance on concrete proposals, which most Americans know nothing about.

This is how the game is played at the moment—with Nepal, Germany, Bolivia, Australia, and any other point on the compass. Israeli Prime Minister Levi Eshkol's visit to President Johnson's ranch home in Texas was a welcome departure from the confines of normal protocol. There the two men could walk out in the sun, project thoughts expansively in a generous time frame with no nervous clock watchers about them. They could watch a sunset together. The Ministers could move in and out of rooms and conversation without tensely held doors, and gold braid guards snapping to attention. It's a better way.

CHAPTER FOUR

Laugh and the world laughs with you is very good advice for most people, though not for a chief of protocol. He must laugh *and* cry alone. On duty he should appear unmoved by events, however hilarious or tragic they may seem. A sense of humor helps as long as it is not displayed. The greatest help, however, is a good-natured sovereign. When he's happy, you're happy. When "we" are not amused, *you* are not amused!

In my two years of service we received seventy heads of state or government, roughly half the world's leaders. Looking back I realize that the processes by which men come to power, and retain it, whether in a royal line, election, or coup, generally equip them with a certain perspective, a kind of patience, a tolerance for departures from the "best laid plans," and a sense of the ridiculous.

When Prime Minister Harold Wilson arrived June 3, 1967, we had every reason to make him and the nation he represented feel supremely welcome and respected. The pound had been devalued. The fundamental decision to withdraw from east of the Suez had been announced. It was farewell to empire, but hello to a nonetheless great Britain. This was an "official visit," the highest category of visit by a head of government. Our President, as aforementioned, is both Head of State and Head of Government, a formidable guest in either capacity. In United States protocol, the only ritualistic feature of a state visit distinguishing it from an official one was for years the brief but gala parade that marked the state visit. This was discontinued recently owing to the difficulty of arousing the citizenry of Washington—for orderly demonstrations, at least. It is a peculiar and lonely feeling to sit in the President's bubbletop with two chiefs of state glumly looking out on empty streets.

In any event, we were determined to make Mr. Wilson's official visit conform in minutest detail to the requirements of protocol. I had conferred with the British ambassador, Sir Patrick Dean, and members of his staff. I had worked long hours with my own staff and the political officers of the State Department, in addition to the White House foreign policy advisers under Walt Rostow. We were ready. The day was cloudless. The helicopter bearing the Prime Minister landed gently on the ellipse in the shadow of the Washington Monument. As the rotors subsided, I approached, met the Prime Minister as he emerged, and escorted him to the waiting limousine. We circled into the drive past the South Lawn. It was lined by the trim honor guard, and enlivened by the presence of some 3000 well-chosen and dutifully cheering federal employees. The Prime Minister leaned back with his feet on the jump seat. He tapped his pipe, and mused aloud, "I wonder how many of our flags are upside down today."

"Surely the Prime Minister is jesting," I replied.

"Not at all," said he; "there's one now. Ah, there's another."

The Union Jack consists of the crosses of England,

Scotland, and Ireland superimposed on a field of blue. The variance in thickness of the white diagonal stripes above and below the flag's center gives a clue as to whether or not it is being flown properly. The thick white stripes should be on the top on the left side, and on the bottom at the right. A number of the boys had it backwards. Prince Charles and Princess Anne encountered the same phenomenon aboard President Nixon's yacht three years later. We do not discriminate in favor of royalty.

The honor guard is under the command of the commanding general of the Military District of Washington. But it is quite clear that when things go wrong in a visit of this kind, Protocol is answerable and must be. The buck stops there. I smiled wanly in disbelief that such a misfortune could have overtaken me so soon in life.

"Not to mind," said the Prime Minister, soothingly; "happens all the time. It is, of course, a signal of distress."

I winced. Nor were my troubles over. We pulled up to the red carpet. I stepped out first, presented Mr. Wilson to the President, and the two stood for an unfortunately long moment in front of one of the errant flags. An enterprising and apparently well-briefed photographer got the picture. This was brought to my attention the next day by a "high source in the government." At 6:30 A.M. the phone rang. It was the familiar Texas voice commending to my interest the front page of the Washington Post. He held the line until I got the paper. There on page one was the picture of the two principals standing beside the upside-down Union Jack, with the caption. "Oops!" "Oops" has been described as the most feared word in surgery. And so it is in protocol. I don't recall my conversation with the

President, or rather his with me, in great detail, but I do remember getting the impression he would have preferred this not to happen, and would not wish it to recur with regularity. I deferred, of course, to his judgment.

I then staggered to the kitchen for a cup of coffee, or possibly hemlock, and opened the paper to the ladies' section, where all truths are revealed. There I saw for the first time the program for the White House entertainment that had been arranged for the visiting Prime Minister that evening. Aware that the visit was taking place against the background of sterling devaluation and withdrawal from the Far East, I gazed incredulously at the proposed repertoire for the proud voice of baritone Robert Merrill: his first selection, "I've Got Plenty of Nuthin' "; his second, "On the Road to Mandalay"; followed by "You'll Never Walk Alone."

These selections, I should point out, were made by the artist himself. The entertainment is chosen by the First Family, and arranged through the office of the social secretary. News management there may have been, but song management, no.

In any event, after seeing what was in the Merrill bag of songs, I placed a call to Sir Patrick Dean. I asked him if he had seen the morning *Post*. He had. I asked if in his view a restructuring of the evening's program might be in order. He "would let me know." In less than a half hour he called back. "Not at all," he said cheerily. "These are all the PM's favorite songs. He hopes he will have a chance to hear them." And so he did, to his own and the President's considerable amusement and the disguised chagrin of the tattered chief. It was late that night that I altered Henley's lines:

Out of the night that covers you
Black as the pit from pole to pole
Thank whatever gods you do
You're not the Chief of Protocol.

I had come to know a good many such chiefs, not only colleagues from abroad, but my own gallant predecessors, Jack Simmons, Stanley Woodward, Wiley Buchanan whom I first met with then Vice President Nixon in London ten years ago, my old friend Angie Duke, Lloyd Hand, and their incomparable wives. It is a great fraternity that lifts its glasses quietly to fallen brethren. Sympathetic vibrations unite its hopes and its anguish. I think of the time the President was received at Canada's Expo '67. In the Place des Nations the Mounties were drawn up in splendid array. Dignitaries stood rank on rank. Five thousand people looked on in awe as the Star Spangled Banner was hoisted to the masthead and unfurled, revealing a hole through the stripes the size of a basketball. I turned to the Canadian protocol officer. He had lost his natural robust coloring. "The flag must come down," he murmured abstractly.

"Why?" I said. "It's flown that way before—that's how we got the song."

With a weak smile he went ahead with instructions to lower the grand old flag. The ceremonies continued. A little old lady was produced. She sat at the foot of the flagpole, sewing furiously. I'll never forget her, still sewing away as the captains and the kings departed, followed by many a smiling diplomat.

Entertainment for our President on his many tours abroad was also varied and fanciful, ranging from the

National Anthem played without reference to the written notes, to the mock savagery of painted Maori tribesmen in New Zealand. Their chief met us at the airport near Wellington, and to the resounding chant of his colleagues, threw the "peace stick" at the President's feet. The President's eyes narrowed. It was his part to pick up the stick and show thereby that he came in peace. The chieftain made loud grunting sounds, and pointed at the stick. He rolled his eyes ominously, with an occasional nervous glance at Prime Minister Keith Holyoake. The latter had attempted to explain the ritual before the jet engines were turned off. Most last minute protocol instructions were given during that period. Consequently, few ever got through. In any case, our President was not of the stick-picking-up kind. I retrieved the stick, and the relieved chieftain gratefully hefted his finger-painted tummy back into the safety of the crowd.

The President then decided to shake hands with all the Maoris standing in a line with feathers, sandals, and war clubs dangling limply. It had been ages since their tribe had eaten a couple of Captain Cook's man. As I followed along, one of the tribesmen grabbed me, and sang in perfect Beatle-inflected English, "I Wanna Hold Your Hand." So much for the Maori warriors.

As a rule we tried during the advance planning to limit ritual to a minimum in order to preserve the President's energy and frame of mind. Official visitors to Washington do have a certain amount to go through, such as the honoring of the Unknown Soldier at Arlington Cemetery, now followed by a visit to President Kennedy's grave. This ceremony is splendid, colorful, and over in thirty minutes. You can get pretty wet in thirty minutes of rain, however, and quite hot in thirty minutes of Washington sun. It is not a required stop, but most visiting sovereigns seem eager to make it, except for those like the Saudi Arabians whose religion forbids this type of public ceremony for the deceased.

For his part President Johnson preferred not to overdo the memorializing. We were well counselled on his penchant for brief ceremonies. In Kuala Lumpur, we were told the Malaysian anthem would be over in two minutes while the President stood at attention. It was over in eight. Standing by the President in the 105-degree heat, I could feel his gaze along that part of my neck which would receive the blade. My head was already bowed out of respect for the dead, and near dead.

Like most of us, the President enjoyed ritual in which he need take no part, especially when it cast his own aides as participants. The presentation of gifts to the King of Malaysia offered just such an opportunity. The President and Mrs. Johnson sat in tufted chairs in a little semicircle with the King and Queen. Leading to the group was a splendid carpet runner, flanked by straight chairs in which sat in bemused silence Secretary Rusk, Assistant Secretary William P. Bundy, Walt Rostow, Marvin Watson, Jack Valenti, Harry McPherson, and others who had only to worry on that trip about what the President should say, not what he should do. I was to present the President's gifts to the King at this time. My role was explained to me with care by the grand chamberlain. It required carrying the gift, a silver cigarette box, on a velvet pillow with measured steps through the gantlet to the King and presenting it to him with a low bow. I was then to stand and walk backward down the carpet out of sight. The

President enjoyed this performance immensely, as did my other fellow-Americans. Mrs. Johnson looked on, as she always did, with great sympathy.

The time to know whether one would do the right thing in the President's eyes was always after the thing was done, not before. Presidential instructions themselves were only to be adhered to if they produced a good result. If not, we should have foreseen the error and made a midcourse correction. This was difficult enough when one had only one's own judgment to rely on, but when decisions of a delicate nature were shared in a mysterious way with one or more others the process was especially complicated. I used to compare the experience to that of a quarterback in a football huddle, with one key difference. In football huddles, the quarterback gives the signals to players who listen silently. In protocol, the chief takes his directions from the other players who all talk at once.

The clearest directive for Presidential advance planning was to avoid home hospitality, often as demanding on the guest as the host. We were to seek the impersonal comforts of hotel accommodation. I felt this to be a particularly good rule for another reason. When the President travels he is not just the man but the institution. Carloads of communications and security equipment must precede him and be installed in his quarters wherever he may be, so that he is never out of touch with the world, and the red phone. Private homes and their owners are likely to be left in a shambles after a visit of that kind. The little rest in the cozy, sunlit bedroom, tea and crumpets, or some other warming refreshment, a chat with the host in the drawing room over a glass of claret—undoubtedly such visions tempt the imaginations of would-be world hosts to the Chief of State of the great American nation.

But if they are so unfortunate as to succeed in their persuasions, what occurs? A dozen burly Yanks, with cords of wire, clippers, hammers, and saws, enter their home with no ceremony at all. They march and countermarch through the hallways. They decide the President will not in fact stay in the sunlit corner room. It's too near the street. As a security precaution, and because he needs two or three bedrooms nearby for staff accommodation, the master bedroom suite would do better, if at all, mind you. A sad beginning, but worse is yet to come. For if the home is approved for the stay—of just a day of two perhaps— walls are drilled, partitions erected, furniture moved, and equipment nailed or screwed in place a week or more in advance, to be removed possibly a week or more later. The Presidency as a house guest is an outsized Eloise.

It wouldn't surprise me to find someday, in some corner of a foreign field that is forever U.S., a paint-chipped abandoned mansion, shutters flapping in the wind, and a creaking sign reading: "The President slept here." Miniaturization of communications equipment should help in time.

Hotels on the other hand are accustomed to guests who do not think of the premises as a home. Moreover, they have no undue sensitivity about billing for damages. With these sobering thoughts in mind I went up to the desk at the hotel in Wellington, an early stop on our six-day advance mission covering the 30,000 miles of the President's Asian trip in October, 1966. The day clerk was an old gentleman, wearing a green visor. He bent over his accounts.

"Hello," I said. "I'm with the American State Department, and I wonder if you could provide some rooms for our President next week."

"No, sir," he replied without looking up.

"For the President," I repeated hopefully.

"Not a thing," said he.

"Why would that be?" I asked.

"Race week," was the terse reply. They were booked up for Race Week. What next? That afternoon I paid a courtesy call on the governor-general of New Zealand, Sir Bernard Fergusson. A long, flower-lined drive led to Government House, an imposing stone residence. I was met in the great hall by a young military aide in a crimson coat. He ushered me into the drawing room. There I settled into a massive wing chair under the awesome gaze of Sir Bernard's lifesize portrait. It appeared he would be a large man, robust, monocled, mustached, and firm. He strode briskly in and confirmed the impression. "Good to meet you," he said, "and good to know the President and Mrs. Johnson will be staying with Lady Fergusson and myself. Jolly good." This was news to me. I thanked Sir Bernard on behalf of the President, and pointed out how the President, not deeming it appropriate to impose on such short notice, had directed us to secure public accommodations. Sir Bernard never took his eyes off me. When I had finished he said very simply, "Impossible. He must, of course, stay with us. If he didn't," he added with a kind of cold finality, "the Queen wouldn't like it." He explained that the farther a Commonwealth country was from Britain, the more sensitive the people were to the royal proprieties. The people of New Zealand "would be injured," he said. Protocol often finds itself between the hammer and the anvil, or, as we say at home, a rock and a hard place. I said I would certainly convey Sir Bernard's kind wishes to the President. "Yes, we'll have none of this hotel nonsense," said Sir Bernard jovially. "We're all set for him, you know."

That evening I related my combined experiences to Bill Moyers, who was in charge of the details of the advance mission. Hotel, no. House, si. Bill was familiar with the hammer but had never met the anvil. "What? You didn't set him straight about the President's preference?" He shook his head goodnaturedly—another softie in the ranks. I said, shucks, and suggested Bill come and straighten out the Governor-General himself.

The two of us went to see him the next day. Again Sir Bernard swept into the room like a nor'easter. "All set for your President," he bellowed. "Lady Fergusson and I— looking forward to it!" Moyers' straightening-out words as I recall were "Yes, sir, the Johnsons are looking forward to it, too, sir." As we drove away Bill turned to me and said, "Quite a man, Sir Bernard." We later learned that Sir Bernard had held a command at Tobruk in a siege that was relieved by Australian troops. As he marched out with his men the Aussies laughed and mimicked his monocle. He halted his men, took out the monocle, flipped it ten feet in the air, and caught it in his eye. "Now you may laugh," he announced, and marched on.

The President received the information without a murmur. Any apprehensions on my part dissolved the moment he saw Sir Bernard and Lady Fergusson. It was a happy household. The President and Mrs. Johnson enjoyed their stay from the outset, when Sir Bernard showed us through the anteroom where guests would gather prior to the evening reception. "The sheep-dip," he explained. I felt Sir Bernard was what the President might have called, "My kind of governor-general." And they did have tea.

The problem of time zone changes deserves a footnote in these reminiscences on the President's seven-nation Asian trip in October, 1966. A person's circadian rhythm, or cycle of sleep and digestion, is naturally disturbed on jet plane trips that propel him through three or more time zones in a given twenty-four-hour period. Traveling on the advance mission, thirty thousand miles by jet in six days, and pausing only one day in Washington before embarking on the same course with the President over a seventeen-day period, brought home to me the seriousness of the problem. Each trip on the way out we were offered breakfast four times in one twelve-hour period. We had to fast when the stomach said "eat" and eat when it cried "not now." A British study with student volunteers of equal aptitude showed poorer performance at simultaneous mental tasks by those flown to India—within forty-eight hours after their arrival—than those who remained in England. Some corporations prohibit the transaction of business by their executives within two days of a jet flight through six time zones. No major decisions should be made, it is argued. The President and his Cabinet, lacking the luxury of accommodating to time changes, made such decisions all along the way.

One antidote for dull lethargy or nervous tension, which the broken circadian rhythm can cause, is exercise. It was a happy coincidence then to have along on the trip such aggressive tennis enthusiasts as Walt Rostow and Harry McPherson. The three of us plus one dragooned embassy man played an hour of doubles at six nearly every morning of the trip. A good sweat first thing in the morning meant a clearer head and steadier gait for the long-houred days.

CHAPTER FIVE

Premier Aleksei Kosygin who came to the UN Special Session in June, 1967, was invited to Glassboro to meet with President Johnson. No official protocol arrangements were made at Glassboro owing to the short notice. On Saturday night, June 24, I was told of the Premier's further plans. The call came from the Defense Department at about 11 P.M. Premier Kosygin had been offered *Air Force II* to go "anywhere he liked" following the Glassboro talks. The Premier had decided on Niagara Falls, and it was my job to get him there.

I had learned it was chancy to commit Presidential amenities without checking with the President personally or with Marvin Watson. Using the White House phone I reached Watson on *Air Force I*, flying west with the President. The answer was, "Sure, and take care of that man."

I then called the Air Force and arranged for the plane to take me to New York at 6 A.M. to wait on the Premier. During the rest of the night I was in telephone contact with the State Department security officers who had gone to Niagara Falls to make arrangements for the Premier's luncheon and visits to various points of interest at the Falls.

We woke the mayor at three o'clock in the morning. His name was Lackey. It seemed amusing at the time to have the honor of presenting the Soviet Premier to an authentic capitalist Lackey. We also woke John, owner of "John's Flaming Hearth," the chosen restaurant. At 5 A.M. I drove to Andrew's Air Force Base and boarded *Air Force II*, a Boeing 707 like its counterpart *Air Force I*, but with a slightly different interior configuration, which I actually preferred owing to the comfortable privacy it offered. The only other passenger was my friend, Assistant State Department Public Affairs Officer David Waters. We arrived in good time and waited expectantly.

At eight o'clock, as we paced the airfield near the plane, a long line of limousines appeared in the distance. As it drew closer it became apparent that Premier Kosygin had brought either a very large farewell party or a good many other fellow-travelers. The latter proved to be the case as the limousines pulled up and discharged the smiling premiers and foreign ministers of Hungary, Czechoslovakia, Bulgaria, and Romania, and a great many premiers of such Soviet Socialist states as Ukraine, Outer Mongolia, and Georgia, plus lesser functionaries. In all, some fifty gentlemen boarded the plane in a never-ending stream. I had greeted Premier Kosygin, Ambassador Anatoliy Dobrynin and Foreign Minister Andrei Gromyko in the vestigial Russian that remained at my command after ten years of shelf life.

As I boarded the plane a few feet ahead of the Premier I noticed on the table beside the seat he would occupy, a copy of *Time* magazine with the headline, "Is Russia the Real Loser in the Mid-East War?" I did not conceive of myself as a news manager, but I wondered if that particular magazine had to be at that particular place at that particular time. I decided it did not and took it away. During the trip the Premier and his associates did seem to find enjoyment from other magazines, particularly the advertisements.

I visited with them till they were settled in, and then went into an aft compartment with some of Kosygin's aides and also his charming daughter, Lyudmila Gvishiani. Her English being a great deal better than my Russian, we had a pleasant conversation all the way to Niagara. We discussed the problems of our two societies in transition from rural to urban life, and the need to preserve man's environment from his ideas of "progress." Mrs. Gvishiani was traveling as her father's hostess, and made the trip pleasant for us all.

Arriving in Niagara, the Premier, a quiet man with a faintly whimsical air about him, immediately found himself in the embrace of Mayor Lackey, a ruddy-faced and jovial gentleman. It was our practice to put ourselves in the hands of local officials to the extent possible and hope for the best. The security men exchanged glances, and I knew they'd had a rough night. From the beginning to the end the Premier's elbow was in the uncompromising grip of Mayor Lackey. His Honor was obliged to let go when we entered the limousine and he and I sat on the jump seats while Premier Kosygin, Ambassador Dobrynin, and Foreign Minister Gromyko settled in the back seat.

As we drove, Premier Kosygin asked me if a visit to the power station was on the agenda. I answered that the power station was not on the agenda but could be placed there. Mayor Lackey assured the Premier that he could indeed visit the power station. Premier Kosygin, with a little smile, said it was interesting that Protocol had not arranged the power station but that the Mayor himself would make that visit possible. I answered that in the haste of the overnight planning we had hoped to emphasize the more romantic aspects of the Falls. The Premier gave a lusty laugh and thumped me on the back. He then asked if the water of the river and the Falls was clean. The Mayor regretted it was not; it was considerably polluted. The Premier was dismayed, and asked why.

"The power station," replied the Mayor.

"Well, something must be done about that," said Premier Kosygin.

I said it did appear the Premier had an interest in preserving the romantic aspects of the Falls. This evoked an even lustier laugh from the Premier and a harder thump on the back.

The Premier must have been familiar with some American political oddities for he asked the Mayor what he did when he was not "being mayor." Mr. Lackey explained he was the public relations consultant for the Carborundum plant.

"What is a public relations adviser?" asked the Premier.

Mr. Gromyko, who had been silent up to that point, said quietly, "He is like a foreign minister."

I laughed and Ambassador Dobrynin laughed, and that was it for laughter.

Arriving at the power station the Premier was escorted into the huge entrance hall featuring Thomas Hart Benton's giant mural of the discovery of Niagara Falls by Father Hennepin surrounded by forward-leaning French soldiers with muskets. The Premier gazed at it a moment, and turned with a deadpan aside to one of his aides, "Everything with cross and gun."

Minor mishaps marked the gallant efforts of power station officials to guide some sixty of us through the entire

plant and up and down in small elevators. Lyudmila asked
if I thought it was necessary for her to see the plant. She
preferred to remain with the crowd in "the fresh air." I
told her she could do exactly that.

The luncheon at "John's Flaming Hearth" was festive.
Because of the language difficulties it was explained that
only two entrees would be served, lobster and steak; steak
could be ordered by slashing one hand across the palm of
the other, and lobster by crooking the finger. The solem-
nity of the old Bolsheviks could not survive the resulting
scene. Abetted by cocktails, the animated gestures contri-
buted to a general relaxation of the party.

As the desserts were cleared, Mayor Lackey rose to welcome Premier Kosygin and his party. The Mayor warmed
to the subject of peace, and assured the Premier that there
were many people all over the United States who saw
avenues to peace that the United States Government failed
to see. The Premier received this intelligence impassively,
as I hope I did. He accepted both the Mayor's words and
the souvenir token of the Falls graciously. He then thanked
his hosts in general, but concluded his remarks by raising
his glass in a toast to "the Chief of Protocol of the United
States who has kept us together in a fine way."

The uncertain value of fluency as a solution to the language barrier was illustrated by the experience of Premier
Kosygin's polite young Soviet interpreter. Becoming separated from the party briefly at Glassboro, he approached
the police lines and stated, in the perfect, unaccented English he had learned in an American university, that he
should be rejoined with the official party. "Yeah, buddy,
move on," said the bemused trooper, experienced in the
wiles of young collegians. Realizing his error, the interpre-

ter approached a trooper farther down the line and made
the same request with a heavy Russian accent. He was admitted at once.

"Be not forgetful to entertain strangers," enjoined St.
Paul in his epistle to the Hebrews. "If a stranger sojourns
in your land," counsels the Torah, "you shall not wrong
him." Solon the lawgiver was put down by a young travel-
ler who told him he had come to make friends with him.
"People should make friends at home," grumbled Solon.
"Then you who are at home make friends with me," replied his uninvited guest.

Mark Twain claimed that he never avoided conversing
with a stranger because the probabilities were that the
stranger could either teach him something or learn something from him. And Will Rogers touched the American
heart when he said he never met a man he didn't like.
But there are those who *will* not meet others they *cannot*
or even *might* not like. They would prefer, in fact, to "get
rid" of them, a mutuality of sentiment that engenders
jihads, Biafras, soap box standoffs between right and left,
and "final solutions."

We don't know ourselves too well, and in a way we
cherish this state of affairs. It provides a fall-back position,
the last refuge for every disputant who would wrest emo-
tional victory from rational defeat by proclaiming his
antagonist could simply "not know" how Moslems feel
about Hindus, Jews about Arabs, Russians about Germans,
Greeks about Turks and Italians, blacks about whites,
North about South, East about West, Flemish about
Walloons, to say nothing of all the vice versas. It is com-

forting that we can manage our affairs at all in the face of an admitted incompetence of this magnitude.

Paradoxically, in America our diversity encourages a tolerance for the other fellow's grudge. There, but for his, goes ours. We stand aside and almost admire it. Some grudges are the transient kind. We reserve them for friends and enemies alike. Old enemies are new friends. Sometimes, sadly, the reverse is true. Still it is the peculiar grace of America, a many-blooded land, to have no blood enemy. But if as Americans we are not "unconsciously in the grip of the past," none of us should consciously encourage minorities or majorities among us to retain their own grip on it. We should not abandon dialogue to the demagogue whose powers grow by default.

The indignant citizen who will tell us "we cannot know how he feels," who jealously guards his secret hate, who taunts us for our failure to perceive it, yet demands we maintain a respectful distance from it, is easy prey to the towering figure astride the white horse or within the white robe who says, "If you feel like I think you feel, fight, burn, kill!" The victim of these persuasions is one moment withdrawn and unapproachable—the cynical guardian of a bitterness he will not share—and the next, a cipher in a howling mob who, following his affair with curses, truncheons, and tear gas, returns to the hearthside of his unfathomable hatred, unmoved.

The cycle can probably be broken by honest inquiry, new friendships, and sacrifices of pride, time, and convenience on the part of the great uninvolved, the silent majority, if you will, who should enter the discussion now, while the better angels of their nature are in control, not later, when they are wrestled down by the self-appointed

ethnarchs of their own respective Old World cultures, or
tempted by the hints of public men seeking short-term
political advantage to give vent to unashamed vindictive-
ness. How people truly feel about one another is not easy
to learn, especially among the silent majority. One can in-
dulge in presumptions along these lines only at considerable risk. But the educated guess is probably the guess one
makes after one gets to know better the people one is
guessing about. The pace of understanding in this country
has been slowed by nonmeetings coast to coast. This is an
area where people can someday lead the government. But
today government should set an instructive example. The
campaign politics of division can achieve a satisfactory,
closely calculated mathematical outcome, but at great cost.
It is easier to lead the nation to that result than to unity
afterward. For to the victor belongs the governance of a
spoiled society.

When a great people arrive at new divisions, the role of
government is to heal them. In today's America there is no
need to create suspicion. There has always been enough to
go around. Nor is there any point in encouraging it. It
grows well enough untended. The role of responsible
leadership is to dispel it. For persons who govern to refer
to "those people," "that certain group" as constituting the
enemies of progress and sanity is to feed the fires of frus-
tration and mutual distrust in the governed. They turn
to their elected and appointed officials for guidance. If an
elected leader, for example, perceives dangers from certain
attitudes and behavior of a powerful person, group, or
sector of the society, he is in a good position to speak directly to them, seek their company, expose his apprehensions, receive their reactions. The process of defusing
antagonisms is really a very direct and personal process,

not an impersonal or indirect one. It is a patently weak gesture to challenge the South in Michigan. Nor should one go to Montgomery, Alabama, to berate *The New York Times*. One goes to the *Times*. Beer hall rhetoric before applauding, uncritical audiences is unworthy enough in a campaign, but it is an extremely injurious manner of governing. Talk, for example, of "trading" people, getting "rid" of people, has to be bewildering to youngsters whose hopes were held high on the placard, "Bring us Together." How indeed can we be brought together and polarized at the same time? How can men become reconciled if they are encouraged to reinforce their biases by the very persons entrusted with the reconciliation? It is the function of American Government to topple violence without enthroning hatred. I concur in President Nixon's inaugural suggestion that voices be lowered. This would include, it must be supposed, voices speaking for him. For any such voices to address mass rallies in uncertain cliches is to feed the fires of resentment on the left and reinforce the hostilities of the vocal right over the silent middle. When America is described as a smaller circle than it is, such political doodling should bemuse no one, but least of all those elected to maintain the circumference.

At any rate, can nonmeetings at home ever really be said to affect our ability to do business abroad? We can examine the question in the light of the visit in 1966 of his Majesty, King Faisal of Saudi Arabia. During the course of this visit two nonmeetings occurred—one between New York and the King, the other between New York and New York. Out of the latter was the former born. The circumstance made me think—fleetingly at least—of the legendary plea made some years ago by a harassed American statesman. Why, he is reported to have asked, cannot the Israelis and the Arabs resolve their differences in a truly Christian spirit?

The spirit of "meeting," of course, is not of Christian invention or discovery. It is a primeval human happening, which finds expression in Judaic, Islamic, Buddhist, and Christian teaching. Could it ever be that the zealous political solicitude of a Christian mayor would misjudge the philosophic commitment of a Jewish constituency? Could he heed, instead, out of a misplaced deference, the representations of ethnic "advisers," whose proxy was revoked years ago by the American experience? We were given an opportunity to put this question and have it answered in the affirmative.

King Faisal had come to America, pursuant to an invitation from the President, on a full state visit. Unlike his predecessor, King Saud, he came with a modest retinue. He wore no jewels. He dressed simply. He spoke quietly. When the horses drawing our Williamsburg carriage bucked at the sight of the helicopter waiting to take us to Washington, he chided the coachman. "It is not proper," he said, "to urge a horse beyond his limits." As he stepped down, curling his robe about him, he continued, "What is more, to these animals the helicopter undoubtedly represents a very large horsefly!"

This was the manner of man who met with the President later in the day and described his new programs for national health and the education of women. That night he enjoyed a splendid state dinner to which, although he had not brought his own wife, ladies were invited with his concurrence. He was at pains throughout not to require or even suggest conformity with the customs of his country.

The following day the King agreed to speak at a luncheon press conference. It was organized by the

Women's Press Club and his Majesty accepted, wanting again to underscore his appreciation of the role of women in American life. It was this conference, more than any other single event of my tenure, that made me realize diplomacy is much too important work to be left to diplomats. Sensitivity and self-restraint are required of every citizen, regardless of his occupation, when he encounters a foreigner. At such times we are all ambassadors, good or bad, but ambassadors nonetheless—even the press.

American politicians are used to the give-and-take of an American press interview. The banter is generally within an accepted context. But it is a strange, new arena for the uninitiated, such as certain kings. A corollary to a familiar axiom would be, "Do not do unto others as you do to yourselves, if you're doing it by the book and you're using a different book." His Majesty explained that the severing of hands for thievery was in fact "by the book." "What is more," he added, "it works."

The audience, a law-and-order crowd, roared its delighted approval of this reply. But the King had not spoken in jest. Then he was asked, "Who is your greatest enemy, Israel or Nasser?"

The King said that the question was hardly proper, that of course Egyptians were Arab brothers and Israelis were not, but that there was no desire to "drive Israel into the sea," only to resolve the Palestine refugee question. "I am a Semite," said the King, "and therefore hardly anti-Semitic." Parenthetically, no press notice was taken of his luncheon remarks the preceding day when he said to his host, Secretary Rusk, and the guests assembled, that the great threat to the Middle East was communism, and that all the "sky" religions, and he named them in this order, "Judaism, Islamism, and Christianity," should cooperate

to keep "communism" out. I thought the statement extra-
ordinarily newsworthy. The press did not. Perhaps they
did not anticipate the Soviet presence in the Mediterra-
nean or SAM sites on the Nile.

The press club luncheon question, however, that trig-
gered the trouble was why businessmen who did business
in Israel were prohibited from doing business in Saudi
Arabia. In reply, the King resorted to an old Arab saying:
"He who helps an enemy is an enemy." If that is an inflammatory statement, it is one made frequently in the halls of
Congress with respect to shipments to North Vietnam. It
is certainly not a newsworthy revelation. The concept is a
reasonable one, and no one doubted that the King's country considered Israel a hostile power. That a power she
was and state she would remain the King had already indicated. And clearly his answer did not mean to imply
that America herself, a helper of Israel, was an enemy of
the King. Some less than perfect judgment went into the
question and some into the answer, but there was still
plenty of room for good judgment in the reactions that followed. There was room for it but it never came.

The somewhat garbled word went out. New York City, a
community of roughly the same size as the visitor's country, certainly acted no larger.

Mayor John Lindsay, a friend and former fellow-
parishioner at St. John's Church, Lafayette Square, pondered his alternatives. He pondered all night, while I
paced the outer halls of the King's chamber at Blair
House, lock step with his advisers in their robes. "How is
it," they asked, "that a municipal leader can overturn the
good will of your President?"

We sat down for coffee as I tried to explain the federal
system and constitutionally limited powers of the Presi-

dent. "He can't make a mayor hold a dinner," I concluded ruefully. It was not comprehensible to the followers of an absolute monarch and keeper of the "holy place" (Mecca) for a hundred million Islamic believers, a hundred million people we wished to convince of our fairness and good faith.

Finally word came—the dinner is canceled. The King's personal attendant went in to inform him, looking briefly back at us, and possibly at his whole life. Moments later he emerged, smiling. "His Majesty is satisfied. There was to be a dinner. Now it has proven inconvenient. His Majesty understands, and will go to New York in any case. He is sure he will find dinner." Thus, through no American agency, a bad situation was prevented from becoming worse. Naturally the controlled Arab press exploded with denunciations and charges that United States policy for the Middle East was made not in Washington but in New York. Public receptivity was established for Nasser's glib charge a year later that American forces were involved in the Six-Day War. So let no one doubt the role of the American citizen in the calm formulation, and effective implementation, of United States foreign policy.

Did the Jews of New York cancel the dinner? It is said that Ambassador Arthur Goldberg opposed the cancellation. Certainly it was not the teaching of the Torah. It was not in the spirit of Martin Buber's "I and Thou" and the need for the two to meet. It was definitely not a sympathetic echo of Israel's own determination to achieve direct talks with Arab leaders.

No, Jewish Americans did not cancel the invitation. Rather, a gentile psychosis about "what Jews want" caused it to be withdrawn—an example of the politics of proxy paranoia. In sleepy haste, a few Anglo-Saxon and Hibernian Janissaries buckled on their armor, scrambled to the battlements, and sounded their protective yawp over the rooftops of New York. It is difficult to retract yawps or to match them with the still, small voice of common sense. So the next morning's announcement that the welcome mat was withdrawn surprised no one.

"Practical politics" was the banter on the Rialto. What was so "practical," I wondered, in the nuclear/jet age, about taking offense or giving it? There was no choice, people shrugged. So as a matter of "practical politics," we joined the handwashers of history in the rest room of choicelessness. President Pompidou's subsequent visit enabled all the players of the Faisal scene to show they hadn't forgotten their parts. But if these were errors they were inevitable errors, considering the nonmeetings that preceded them. For what the Jewish American "wants"— in common with all Americans—is a just peace in the world. Nor are a people, animated by the teachings of the Old Testament, likely to believe such a peace and the great conversation in which mankind is engaged to that end can be well served by slammed doors, turned-off hearing aids, and turned-away strangers. Any "politics" that result in such phenomena can safely be characterized as "impractical." Israel, in fact, herself desires direct talks with Arab countries. Are we saying they are not necessary? What if the Mayor had called on New Yorkers to receive the President's guest and show him what manner of people we are? Would that have cost him his reelection three years hence? And, if it would, what kind of people are we, indeed? Are we not the peacemakers, the ecumenicists, the one people liberated from Old World hang-ups?

Yet when a Moslem religious leader, who also happened to be a King, gave voice to an interfaith alliance in the context of Middle Eastern policy, his words were ushered into obscurity by the indifference of a press and public, which preferred to snicker at the Punch-and-Judy dilemma of a Christian Mayor "caught" between Jew and Arab.

While we laugh and live out this neo-Medieval cartoon, Communist Russia, which has already arranged one interim accommodation between Hindu and Moslem neighbors, waits for further defaults on the part of the West to expand the Spirit of Tashkent or to cement an ever more radicalized Arab world to its cause. The Middle East is said to be the cradle of civilization. Will it also be its grave? No American President should be the scapegoat for historical processes that transcend the reasonable limits of his authority, that rest, in fact, on implacable hatreds that he cannot soften. They, the dark side of the human spirit, require the ministrations of men committed to spiritual understanding. A plague then on all our temples if their actual function, as communism claims, is to keep man and man apart.

No, if we would grasp the outstretched hands about us, if we would but "entertain the strangers" in our life— then we could together unfurl once and for all that unmistakable banner that has bewitched the world: The Spirit of America.

CHAPTER SIX

Whether or not nations end up on "our" side can well depend on how we treat their sovereigns. King Faisal's patience survived his experience here. Unshaken by our impolitesse, recently he has demonstrated a more flexible attitude toward the resolution of the Mideast crisis.

Normally, we don't have visiting sovereigns to impress or depress, as the case may be, but we certainly do have their representatives. In Washington, between state visits, the continuing concern of Protocol is the welfare of the Diplomatic corps. Following the ceremony marking my appointment, the President and I stood for a moment in the Rose Garden squinting into the sun for the commemorative photo. The President turned to me and said, "You know what a constituency is?" I thought I did. "Well, I want you to think of the diplomats in Washington as your constituency." By serving them, said the President, "you will be serving me." It was a clear enough mandate.

There are over two thousand accredited diplomats in Washington, representing some 120 nations. A diplomat is not, as one irreverent characterization states, "an honest gentleman sent abroad to lie for his country." The job of a diplomat is to represent, report, and negotiate; that is, to represent his government to the government and people of the host country, to report his observations, insights, and suggestions to his own government, and to participate in certain discussions and negotiations between the two governments. A country, as diverse, busily preoccupied, and essentially indifferent as the United States, is a major challenge for the talents of the most seasoned foreign diplomat. Yet many arrive without such seasoning. Their wives and families may need guidance as well. Years ago, long before my appointment to Protocol, my wife with a few friends paid calls on the wives of newly appointed diplomats from "emerging" nations. One was sitting on the floor of an unfurnished apartment watching television. Another, speaking only French, had a severe toothache, and didn't know how to contact a dentist. My wife took her to ours, and served as interpreter. There were later visits of this kind to a hairdresser, a drug store, a supermarket.

By the time of my Protocol appointment, few diplomatic families needed this kind of attention. But it is one thing to know how to survive in Washington and quite another to do an effective representational job. To this end we tried to improve the relationships of the Diplomatic corps with the Congress, the press, and the public —in addition, of course, to the President and the Executive branch generally. This "bridge-building" responsibility was one which we in Protocol shared with other offices and sections of the State Department, from assistant secretaries of state to the "desk officers" who keep in touch with developments in their respective, assigned countries. To those who find it convenient to ascribe the nation's ills to "that State Department," I can say I never worked with finer people.

The relationship between Congress and the Diplomatic corps has not been characterized by the warmest kind of mutual respect and trust. It might be no great exaggeration to suggest that each has considered the other a necessary evil. They are a little awed by each other, which is neither helpful nor necessary. With apologies to shoes that don't fit, I would say that to the composite congressman the composite diplomat is a pasteboard fellow, a striped-pants, cookie-pushing hustler, illegally parked. To the diplomat the congressman is a widely uninformed fellow with a crusty disposition except when he laughs at the wrong time. The wives and women principals, on the other hand, get on well. They are, in fact, the most effective catalysts in dissolving these imagined and, needless to say, distorted stereotypes. Experimenting with ways to close the breach, I devoted an evening in 1966 to a joint reception for young diplomats and congressmen. I invited, with their wives, the five youngest Democratic members of the House and their five youngest Republican colleagues to the State Department auditorium. There were about 800 junior diplomats. Each congressman was asked to prepare a three-minute address on his district—why he ran, why he won—without being serious. The young legislators were no disappointment. John Tunney of California, John Culver of Iowa, Frank Brasco of New York, Bill Steiger of Wisconsin, Don Riegle of Michigan, and the others each bravely mounted the stage, faced the flowing robes, saris and keen curiosity of a highly sophisticated young audience, and did themselves proud. After the presentation we adjourned for coffee, and visited with these representatives from fifty or more countries. It was good for tomorrow's congressional leaders to meet tomorrow's ambassadors, foreign ministers, perhaps Presidents. They had nothing to lose but their preconceptions, and possibly they had a world to save. It will take time, and a certain cautious alchemy, to achieve the necessary trust, not only between Congress and *foreign* diplomats but also between Congress and our own.

Prior to the debate on the foreign aid bill in 1969, I was amazed by the absence of direct contact of House members by State spokesmen. When the debate ended and the bill passed with the oddest assortment of cuts, additions, and declarations of intent—all quite contrary to the larger purposes of any Administration past or present—I could hazard a surmise on this lack of departmental guidance. After some two decades of observing reason dethroned, the department simply stands prayerfully by while Congress works its "will," which is to say, its whim. State's reaction might be compared to that of the family of a missionary who has been both captured and injured by the tribe he sought to civilize, and whose wounds are being treated by the tribal witch doctor. They cannot affect either the treatment itself or the blasphemous incantations that accompany it. So they simply stand aside and silently entreat their own deity.

But, regarding the welfare of the Diplomatic corps in Washington, we cannot stand aside. The plight of embassies old and new seeking expanded or more modern quarters required working with the Congress in another way, as well as with the Metropolitan D. C. Planning Commission, local architects and developers, and the General Services Administration. The long and tedious effort to secure a new permanent site for the Organization of American States, with additional space for a dozen or more new embassies, required the support of congressional leaders, testimony before Congressman Kenneth Gray's Subcommittee on Public Works, and pilgrimages to Senators Wayne Morse, J. W. Fulbright and John Sparkman. After an appraisal of competing sites, a government tract, formerly occupied by the Bureau of Standards, was selected. Long walks and talks with the Latin delegates who would occupy the new premises secured their approval as well. Self-styled spokesmen for alternate plans treated us to a lively series of visitations. We were exposed to the full panoply of pressures and influences that can be brought to bear when large parcels of real estate are involved. We set a straight course and made port.

I had less luck with an extracurricular endeavor that I believed and still believe important to the enhancement of our Diplomatic relations in Washington. Of the two thousand or more diplomats and families, only a few enjoy the privilege of club relaxation, recreation, and entertainment. This is due to three factors: (1) saturation of existing facilities and long waiting lists, (2) prohibitive fees and dues, and (3) ethnic restrictions. American diplomats abroad do not encounter equivalent difficulties. We can see why such amenities are important when we realize the encouragement we otherwise give to the notion that convivial social association is the norm in American living. An American experience, therefore, which denies our guests access to the norm, tends to reduce both their confidence in themselves and their esteem for us. Secondly, Americans are known to do business together in such pleasant circumstances. Yet what more important "business" is there than peace? A third benefit that would derive from establishing a rural retreat for seminars, golf, tennis, and entertainment would be the implicit acceptance for membership and participation of nonwhite Americans as well as foreign diplomats.

I learned of one or two foundations, anxious to further the purposes of United States foreign policy, that might have subsidized memberships for modest-salaried American officials with relevant duties in the international field. The memberships would follow the jobs, and become transferred to succeeding appointees for example, the new "desk officer" for Afghanistan following his predecessor's transfer to the field. Because of the contemptuous and undiplomatic delight with which I'm sure the general idea would have been received by congressional appropriations authorities, I concentrated exclusively on the private sector for help in underwriting what would be regarded as a "country club" in spite of its "spin-off" benefits. It was after I came to Congress that I learned of attempted arrangements to establish a segregated golf club for a small southern community with FHA financing. I would not have thought such an arrangement remotely possible even for an unsegregated community serving the world community.

As protocol chief, looking for private initiatives, I visited leaders and representatives of the international business community and the foundations. McGeorge Bundy was bemused by the idea, but could not commit the Ford Foundation to an investment in real estate. I found some sites, toured them with interested ambassadors, and raised some money, but not enough. Big hopes were dashed. And a vivid anachronism, the absence of a place for summer and winter recreation for diplomats in the capital of the free world, continues. The real losers are the "host" government, the people it represents, and the policies it would promote. Due to conceptual failures of this kind, as well as the social inertia of a self-satisfied community, opportunities to meet and know foreign diplomats are too infrequent, too structured, and too brief.

At present the best way to learn what the ambassadors accredited to the United States are thinking, or perhaps worrying about, is to visit them on their own ground. The chief of protocol has the opportunity, if not the duty, to attempt this. A newly arrived ambassador is normally met at the airport or other entry point by an assistant chief of protocol. At an early opportunity the new arrival pays a courtesy call on the chief of protocol at which time arrangements are made for his introduction to the secretary of state. Secretary Rusk had an easy way of drawing out each new ambassador. A grandfather clock stood in the corner of his office, ticking quietly, giving the impression of patient endurance with all that had passed and of steadfastness for the future. With his humor, sensitivity, and Georgian manner, the Secretary gave more than that. He would invariably recall some pleasant connection with the ambassador himself, his home, or some mutual friend. He would ask after the new man's family, how many children, what ages, and conclude by assuring him that his "door would be open at any time," and that he "and Ambassador Symington" were at his service. Although "no matters of substance" was the rule for these courtesy calls, the Secretary knew exactly when and how to adhere to or depart from that rule.

A copy of the letters of credence and recall, by which a foreign sovereign notifies our President of the recall of his former ambassador and his appointment of a replacement who also enjoys his full confidence, is left with the secretary during this call, as are the ambassador's "remarks," prepared for delivery upon his presentation to the President, but not spoken on that occasion. They and the "letters" are merely exchanged in envelopes for the President's welcoming "remarks." Following the call on the secretary, arrangements are made for the White House presentation.

Secretary Rusk did not admit to being amused by many things, but he took particular satisfaction from letters of credence, which assured the President of their authors' full confidence in the new ambassador and concluded cryptically, "and I commend you to the protection of the Almighty."

One problem for me was that most of the corps were old hands by the time I came on the scene. Yet it was important to know them as well as, or better than, the new arrivals. For this reason I embarked on a program, not required by custom, of calling on every ambassador at his own embassy, starting with the dean of the corps himself, the affable and generous Ambassador of Nicaragua, Dr. Guillermo Sevilla-Sacasa. Baron Louis Scheyven of Belgium was the second in line and frequently stood in for the heavily engaged Dean. Both men were of great help to me.

These calls took time. It was impossible to complete the list in two years owing to other demands, including the scheduled seventy visits and some unscheduled ones. But I considered the chance to visit informally with these men one of the most enriching experiences of my tour. I learned more clearly the hidden dimensions of each man who had made diplomacy his career. Diplomacy is creative work. It was no surprise then to find extremely creative persons engaged in it and drawn to those who made it their profession.

Ambassador Alexander Matsas of Greece, courtly and

handsome, represented not only his country but one of its greatest legacies to the Western world. His poetry and plays are luminous and touching. I called on him to discuss problems of the Greek Embassy and ended up reading his *Croesus* aloud over a glass of *ouzo*.

A foreign service officer has attended so many ceremonies and raised his glass to so many persons, achievements, and speeches, that they may, and possibly should, pass from his mind in time. Yet some of these occasions cannot be forgotten. Such was the presentation by Ambassador Matsas of a Greek helmet found at the site of the battle of Marathon. On the anniversary of the Truman Doctrine he asked that Dean Acheson, to whom he handed it, convey it to the former President with the thanks of Greece. The Ambassador told with a poet's feeling what the battle (490 B.C.) meant to Western civilization, and what Truman's bold decision meant for Greece. The bronze helmet, with its graceful lines and hollow eyelets, seemed to say what could not be said. For a fleeting moment we had the sensation of being joined in purposes that transcended the ages.

The current Greek ambassador is said to be a violinist of concert caliber. It is in the tradition, even while democracy burns in its old cradle.

But diplomatic culture, like history, neither begins nor ends with Greece. Washington has been enriched by the paintings of Ambassadors Alexandre Ohìn of Togo and Fernando Ortuño of Costa Rica, and the accomplished musicianship of Ambassadors Egidio Ortona of Italy and Arne Gunneng of Norway.

The Peruvian Embassy's collection of primitives from Cuzco and pre-Columbian silver had no peer in Washington. If the diplomats bring much to Washington in the way of talent, their judgment is further illustrated by the wives they chose. Gifted pianists include Mrs. Anatoliy Dobrynin, wife of the Soviet ambassador, and Mrs. D. A. De Silva, wife of the Ceylonese first secretary. Mrs. Olavi Munkki, the Finnish ambassador's wife, is a superb potter. The wife of the former Ceylonese ambassador, Mrs. Oliver Weerasinghe, has sung and narrated professional albums celebrating the folk traditions of many lands.

A small Steinway piano now graces Blair House, the President's guest house. It permanently replaced one installed hastily in preparation for the visit of the Philippine President. We knew the beautiful Mrs. Ferdinand Marcos was a singer of great talent, and would wish to practice her songs for the Philippine return reception for President and Mrs. Johnson. Following this visit, my wife reported to Steinway Brothers this void in the Blair House collection. Within weeks it was filled.

A noted broadcaster and radio commentator is Mrs. Abdul Hamid Sharaf, wife of the Jordanian ambassador. She had met President Nixon before most of her colleagues, having interviewed him on his trip to Jordan during his vice presidency. Mrs. Jerzy Michalowski, the Polish ambassador's wife, is a noted writer as is the novelist Baroness Scheyven, wife of the former Belgian ambassador.

Some of the ladies vie professionally with their husbands in the field of diplomacy. The wife of former Ambassador Avrahm Harman of Israel, served at the UN and currently directs Israel's Commission on Demography. Others give generously of their time and interest to civil and charitable causes throughout Washington.

The few names above, a very incomplete list, merely

suggest the abundance of skill and creativity that distinguishes the Diplomatic corps in Washington and undoubtedly throughout the world. To discover this creativity was to see more clearly and hopefully the road we travel as people rather than as chessmen maneuvering for advantage.

While we admired the diplomats as individuals, their music, art and literature, we had to be ever mindful of the customs and rules by which they expected to be treated as representatives of sovereign powers.

CHAPTER SEVEN

Keeping the order of official precedence up to date has been an important function of foreign ministries since its outlines were confirmed by the Congress of Vienna in 1815. Periodically, prior to that time, scrimmaging among ambassadors in streets and entrances tended to lower the level of diplomatic contact. The doorways of some London houses were actually widened so that two or more envoys could enter abreast, scowling, but not scuffling. Diplomatic temperament has cooled over the centuries. Still I know from experience that being at the very end of a line has its hazards. When the *Nautilus* completed its polar submersion in 1958 it docked in Portsmouth, England, where it was met by the town dignitaries, including the Lady Mayoress, as well as the American ambassador and his aide, me. For the anthems, we were invited aboard and lined up according to rank. This put me at the end of the line, and behind the Lady Mayoress. The deck of a submarine is narrow. My heels hung over the edge. If I were to have lost my balance, it would have been instinctive to grab the Lady Mayoress, undiplomatically. I was grateful then for the martial spirit of the occasion, which required the generously endowed woman to stand rigidly erect. If she had relaxed, and I had gone

in, it would have been strictly in accordance with protocol. Like the horizontal guardsmen annually felled by
heat prostration during the trooping of the colors, I
should have been ignored, as I floated off at attention.

Three centuries earlier an incident nearly led to a serious rupture in relations and a threat of war. In 1661 the
coaches of the Spanish and French ambassadors to England were jockeying for position behind the royal coach.
The accompanying footmen and retainers fought. The
Spanish prevailed. When the news reached France, King
Louis XIV ousted the Spanish ambassador and demanded
the French cortege precede the Spanish in every official
procession.

For the next 154 years things must have been in a state
of uneasy flux. At the Congress of Vienna the French did
better, Talleyrand regaining diplomatically a co-equal
status that France had then recently lost in the field.

In addition to its various political settlements the Congress established ambassadorial precedence on the basis
of seniority at the post concerned. The United States
Office of Protocol is charged with keeping our Diplomatic list, the "blue book" list of diplomats accredited to
the United States, current and accurate. An ambassador-
designate may land in July and motor to Washington that
same month. But if he waits to present his credentials ten
minutes after a colleague who arrives in September, he is
enrolled behind him. Knowledgeable ambassadors, therefore, are quite anxious to be received at once.

In the two years I served, I presented some sixty new
ambassadors to the President. In one case the presentation was delayed because of a telephone call from the
State Department early on the designated morning
informing me that the new ambassador had unwittingly

been in contact with a leper over the preceding week. It was not yet apparently necessary for him to know this, nor did it seem appropriate to advance it as a reason for postponing the presentation. I reported the President was unavoidably detained. Luckily no other presentations were made that day.

The rule in my time—the President's pleasure, that is —was that no ambassador should wait more than ten days in Washington before presenting his credentials, and that ambassadors should, as far as possible, be brought to the White House in groups for rapid successive individual presentation and a joint "informal" meeting. This saves the President's time, but is a highly unsatisfactory procedure, as most ambassadors would privately attest. Although nothing of substance is to be taken up during the brief, informal coffee that follows the presentation, it is awkward to have three or four ambassadors from different cultures, climes, and politics, all leaning forward nervously, some with interpreters, trying to savor the offhand pleasantries of the world's most potent Chief of State. But what could be suggested and what insisted upon are two different things when the beneficiary of one's wisdom is the President.

We were able to separate certain Middle Eastern emissaries and other combustible combinations, but it took a reasoned memo, signed and approved by the secretary of state and a White House "adviser" to accomplish it safely.

The "order of precedence," that is, the ranking of officials, should be observed at all *official* functions. The planning for private functions, dinners, etc., should bear it in mind as suggestive but not obligatory. The order of precedence, all the way *down* to the chief of protocol, the last time I looked, was as follows:

TABLE OF PRECEDENCE

The President of the United States
The Vice President of the United States
The Speaker of the House of Representatives
The Chief Justice of the United States
Former Presidents of the United States
The Secretary of State
The Secretary-General of the United Nations
Ambassadors of Foreign Powers—individually ranked by
    order of date of presentation of credentials
Widows of former Presidents of the United States
United States Representative to the United Nations
Ministers of Foreign Powers (Chiefs of Diplomatic Missions)
Associate Justices of the Supreme Court of the United States
    and Retired Associate Justices
The Cabinet
  The Secretary of the Treasury
  The Secretary of Defense
  The Attorney General
  The Postmaster General
  The Secretary of the Interior
  The Secretary of Agriculture
  The Secretary of Commerce
  The Secretary of Labor
  The Secretary of Health, Education, and Welfare
  The Secretary of Housing and Urban Development
  The Secretary of Transportation
The Senate
Governors of States (unless the function in question occurs
    in a Governor's own State, in which case he ranks after
    the Vice President)
Former Vice Presidents of the United States
The House of Representatives
Charges d'affaires of Foreign Powers

The Under Secretaries of the Executive Departments and
the Deputy Secretaries
Administrator, Agency for International Development
Director, United States Arms Control and Disarmament
Agency
Secretaries of the Army, the Navy, and the Air Force
Director, Office of Management and Budget
Chairman, Council of Economic Advisers
Chairman, Board of Governors, Federal Reserve
Chairman, Joint Chiefs of Staff
Chiefs of Staff of the Army, the Navy, and the Air Force
(ranked according to date of appointment)
Commandant of the Marine Corps
(5 Star) Generals of the Army and Fleet Admirals
The Secretary-General, Organization of American States
Representatives to the Organization of American States
Director, Central Intelligence Agency
Administrator, General Services Administration
Director, United States Information Agency
Administrator, National Aeronautics and Space Administration
Administrator, Federal Aviation Administration
Chairman, Civil Service Commission
Chairman, the Atomic Energy Commission
Director, Defense Research and Engineering
Director, Office of Emergency Planning
Director, the Peace Corps
Director, Office of Economic Opportunity
Special Assistants to the President
Deputy Under Secretaries
Assistant Secretaries of the Executive Departments
United States Chief of Protocol

It was always a humbling reminder to read over this list.

On one Sunday in August, 1966, I had to recall an important variance. It was just before dinner on the U.S. cruiser *Northampton*, Canada-bound for a joint meeting with Prime Minister Lester Pearson and dedication of the Roosevelt Cottage Memorial at Campobello. Senators and congressmen were aboard with their wives, as well as Governor John Reed of Maine. They were to dine in the President's suite, seated according to rank. Remembering that a governor in his state outranks all but the President and vice president, I had only to determine it, at the beginning of dinner at least, we were still in the territorial waters of Maine. We were. Nor did it seem necessary to plan a switch at dessert time.

Looking again at the list, we should note the placing of the secretary-general of the United Nations—above the ambassadors. Prior to 1967 he had been placed after the last of the ambassadors, because each of them personally represented a sovereign state, and he did not. Secretary Rusk was disturbed by the inherent anomaly of placing the United Nations secretary-general behind the most recently arrived ambassador. Ambassador Arthur Goldberg had registered his disapproval as well. It was suggested that the secretary-general be placed immediately before the ambassadors, with the rationale that each nation represented had delegated so much sovereign power to the United Nations as to make it a viable political entity. Taken together, this cumulation of "ceded" world sovereignties justified a symbolic recognition of this kind. This seemed particularly important if the United Nations was ever to be accorded the respect necessary for it to function as a competent alternative to the melange of power politics that had brought the world to the brink of extinction. Of course, in protocol, as in the legal profession, hard cases make, if not "bad law," at least difficult rules to administer. For example, the placing of the presidents of the General Assembly and Security Council becomes a delicate process, especially in the presence of dignitaries from countries that don't accord equivalent status to United Nations officials.

Regarding the listing as a whole, it should be reemphasized it is for observance at official functions only. It is not required at private occasions. Moreover, there are certain personages who because of age, renown, or former connection, are considered *dehors*, "outside," of protocol, and seated with appropriate respect and without prejudice. In this category certainly is the lovely and gracious Mrs. Alice Longworth, who is not only the daughter of President Theodore Roosevelt and the widow of Speaker of the House Nicholas Longworth, but also a noted Washington hostess in her own right. The average diplomat would not object to this and, to my mind, none has in recent times, but prior to my service in Protocol, a noted European ambassador did assume offense at such an arrangement and left the dinner. It was not an act that served to enhance an otherwise estimable career. Coming to the aid of a party may require eating in the kitchen. I did so during the state dinner of Italy's President Guiseppe Saragat. A last minute addition to the guest list made a dropout necessary. I was joined in the kitchen by Bess Abell and Presidential Assistant Joe Califano who, in Roman deference to the spirit of the occasion, raised his glass in a toast and emptied its contents on my shirt. I forget the vintage, but it was a red. My eye fell on a White House staffer roughly my size. He knew what to do. Moments later in his shirt I attended the two Presidents during their less eventful toasts.

One advantage of group meetings with newly presented ambassadors was that if one beneficiary of the
President's attention lost his voice or the thread of the
conversation in the magic of the moment, the host could
turn to another and begin anew. On one occasion a new
ambassador from Central Europe extolled his country's
blueberries. Through an interpreter he pronounced them
"magnificent." Weeks later at a diplomatic reception he
gingerly approached me with a sad look. He had made,
he said, a great mistake in his meeting with the President.
I assured him I was conscious of no error at all.

"No," he replied, "I told the President about our blueberries. I had meant to say strawberries! Terrible. I don't
know what to say!"

I didn't want to overreassure him by suggesting the
President might not have filed that misinformation for
further reference. I said rather that the President, a great
"berry" man, would be grateful for the clarification.

Stage fright afflicted very few diplomats and, as I
recall, only one sovereign, the leader of a newly-emergent
state. The President, leaning back in his rocker, asked him
how he enjoyed Washington. The visitor, a portly gentleman, opened his mouth, and made a breathing sound. He
became wide-eyed and tried again but could muster only
a kind of aimless sigh. The President asked him to pull up
a little closer and repeat that. With little hitching movements the visitor moved over. The President was quiz-
zically looking down the man's throat during the second
attempt, lacking only a tongue depressor to complete the
picture of a concerned country doctor. Then he shook
his head sadly and turned to me.

"Enjoying his visit tremendously," I said. As the President leaned back in slack-jawed comprehension, the

visitor nodded gratefully. I then explained the day's schedule, looked at my watch, and with the President's evident approval helped the stricken visitor to his feet and out past the stern visage of Marvin Watson, the President's executive assistant.

"You'll have to do better with your people," Marvin told me later. My poor people.

Some visitors needed no conversational warm-up or Presidential encouragement. The Emperor of Ethiopia, Haile Selassie, for example, who has known the White House under six Presidents, arrived for an exchange of views with President Johnson. The President's participation was confined to a greeting and farewell. The hour and a half between was consumed effortlessly by the Lion of Judah and his tireless interpreter. I can't say that this was precisely the approach one would counsel for an audience with Lyndon Johnson. But interrupting Emperors is an acquired habit, and I hadn't acquired it.

One matter which seldom presented problems was the visitor's dress. We were used to robes, jodhpurs, skirts, sashes, and swords. It was the ordinary business suit of a certain royal visitor from the East that gave momentary concern. As the limousine pulled up at the red carpet, and I was preparing to vault out the door, I noticed that the visitor was in a serious, though not yet critical, state of undress. He was unsmiling. With seconds to go I had to decide whether to break the news. To do so might induce a state of inopportune panic. Surely he was more at ease being inscrutable. Yet if I said nothing? Our motto in Protocol was, "When in doubt, do the right thing." Very helpful. I saw that his jacket was double-breasted and long. If he stood, it should conceal the difficulty, unless caught in some way. I had been a pretty good chief of protocol all week. I figured I deserved a break. I said nothing. The visitor sprang from the limousine, turned, and faced the cameras, inscrutably. The jacket performed its noble function. Some tailor out there, I thought, likes me. The two leaders exchanged speeches, reviewed the troops, and shook hands. The rest was coasting. We drove to Blair House where I saw him to his rooms. Perhaps he was moved to reflection at that time.

Preventing and, if necessary, absorbing the embarrassment of others is the natural mandate of a protocol officer. No embarrassment is trivial when the wrong persons suffer it, yet some are less trivial than others. It is discomfiting, for example, to have one's embassy robbed, stoned, or bombed, one's person molested, and one's children beaten at, or on the way to, school. Yet these things happened with regularity on Embassy Row. The Office of Protocol has an assistant for special services, a euphemistic expression meaning Diplomatic problems of every kind from real estate and school placement to law enforcement. I consulted frequently with the chief and deputy chief of the Washington police force in an effort to make good my pledge to the dean of the Diplomatic corps that we would increase embassy protection. As a matter of international law and custom the persons and property of Diplomatic missions are to be rendered inviolate by the host government. This responsibility can't be delegated away. Yet we were a long way from conforming, as the Italian ambassador whose butler was shot, the Yugoslav ambassador whose embassy was bombed, and the Kuwait ambassador who was robbed in his bedroom would attest.

Many burglaries, robberies, and assaults on Diplomatic personnel go unreported for two reasons—fear of additional reprisals and the loss of dignity that the publicity entails. Nor are reported offenses necessarily prosecuted. The Italian Ambassador Sergio Fenoaltea did not wish his wounded butler to chance humiliation on the stand at the hands of a clever defense attorney. The indignity, particularly if no conviction were obtained, would be shared by the whole embassy and the country it represented.

A number of United States ambassadors abroad are protected by troops or special guards. The recent assignment of an enlarged White House police force to Embassy Row may do the job here. At any rate it is a federal, that is to say, a national responsibility, which can't be fobbed off on an overburdened local police force. My internal memorandum to this effect darkened an in-box or two if it was not confined to the circular file. Protocol does not take its problems to the public. Perhaps it was found after I left because President Nixon did undertake to strengthen the White House security staff and assign it the additional responsibility of embassy protection, as welcome a move as it is overdue.

On the gentler side, the contributions of wives of chiefs of protocol should be more noted and longer remembered. My wife, like many an unheralded lady before and since, had the nearly full-time task of working with and for the wives of foreign ambassadors and government leaders. Under protocol, the wife assumes the rank of her husband even when he is not present. With White House Social Secretary, our good friend, Bess Abell, Sylvia presented ambassadors' wives to Mrs. Johnson at a series of teas, and helped the unfamiliar new arrivals become oriented to Washington life. During their visits to this country, she also served as escort to the Queen of Thailand, the Queen of Nepal, Princess Lala Aicha of Morocco, Princess Alexandra of Great Britain, Madame Indira Ghandi of India, Madame Ne Win of Burma, Mrs. Takeo Miki and Mrs. Eisaku Sato of Japan, Mrs. Kurt Kiesinger of Germany, Mrs. Ferdinand Marcos of the Philippines, Mrs. Zalman Shazar and Mrs. Levi Eshkol of Israel, Mrs. Gustavo Díaz Ordaz of Mexico, Mrs. Otto Krag of Denmark, Mrs. Mohamed Ibrahim Egal of Somalia, Madame Félix Houphouët-Boigny of the Ivory Coast, and the lovely Greek sisters, Princess Irene, a distinguished young pianist, and Princess Sophia, wife of Prince Juan Carlos. He and their brother, Constantine of Greece, are monarchs for our time, thoughtful and good-natured young men with their own perspectives of the generation gap and the crises of confidence, which stir the young world and shake the old.

Separate schedules, made up for the ladies, were generally predicated on the traditional sorority of feminine interest. A few, like Mrs. Lee Kuan Yew of Singapore, a double first at Oxford, who ranked ahead of her brilliant husband in class, in Women's Lib fashion, sought out American writers and jurists in addition to school children, hospitals, and museums.

Although the published customs and interests of forthcoming visitors were studied in detail, important footnotes would occasionally be overlooked. My wife planned a luncheon at Blair House for the wife of a visitor from the East. Mrs. Rusk was the hostess. The guest of honor spoke some English but neither her ladies-in-waiting nor the wife of her ambassador spoke a word. Accordingly, we had arranged for a Peace Corps volunteer to serve as a noneating interpreter in the somewhat exotic tongue involved. He was banned, however, from the dining room by a last minute edict of the visitors' chief of protocol. There was no opportunity to explain why. The luncheon was pleasant, but not much enlivened by conversation. Later my wife found the abashed Peace Corpsman and asked for what good reason he had not made his appearance. He explained that under the visitors' law, a chief of protocol who permitted a strange man to be alone with the guest of honor would have had his ears cut off.

"That," said my wife, "is a good reason."

One of the advantages of British visitors is that they do not demand the tails and ears of erring protocol officers. And while they expect a certain standard of performance, they may even acknowledge it. Thus on my arrival with Ambassador John Hay Whitney on a 1958 visit to Manchester, I overheard the Lord Mayor express pleasure at having "Ambassador Winant" as his guest. Whitney hadn't heard him. John Gilbert Winant, Ambassador to England during World War II, was deceased. I approached the Lord Mayor and told him how happy Ambassador *Whitney* was to be invited. The Lord Mayor blinked and nodded. At dinner he toasted the United States, Ambassador Whitney, and me, without explaining the dividend. Two years of service in our London embassy gave me useful insights into the often delicate management aspects of an ambassador's job.

Violations of law by embassy personnel that became matters of public record reflect on the whole corps, reduce public respect, and raise the wrath of Congress. A prime example is the annual congressional outcry over the hundreds of unpaid Diplomatic parking tickets. This problem underlines the need to provide ample areas for Diplomatic activity. But it cannot always be presumed that in an altercation with a local citizen or law officer the diplomat's version of events is invariably correct. The promise of immunity frequently tempts the less fastidious diplomat to seek other advantages as well, such as suprior credibility. A traffic violation by a United Nations diplomat in New York gave rise to an irate call on me by his country's ambassador to Washington. A complete apology and reprimand of the arresting officer were demanded. I investigated the matter, I learned the diplomat had run a red light, refused to produce identification, and driven off with the officer's arm caught in the window. I called on the ambassador and presented the facts. The man was sent home shortly. It is good that other indiscretions involving paternity suits and shoplifting charges are dealt with quietly.

CHAPTER EIGHT

The Office of Protocol is a relatively new division in the United States Department of State. Nineteenth-century Presidents generally approached the matter with a some-time conformity to European models punctuated with periodic overlays of Presidential individualism. Jefferson, it is said, attempted to do away with social distinctions, while Zachary Taylor's rough-and-ready disregard of amenities resulted in a sharp exchange of notes with France.

A ceremonial unit was established to handle the 1919 visit of Belgium's King Albert in thanks for our participation in his nation's deliverance. It languished during the post-war years as we once again turned away from world responsibilities. It was Secretary Frank Kellogg's Order 434, February 4, 1928, that established the permanent Division of Protocol. The visit of King George and Queen Elizabeth in 1939 confirmed its function in the planning and execution of state visits, and demonstrated their relevance to policy. It was clear the visit was proposed and accepted as a message to Britain's enemies, colonies, and friends.

The office today, with a staff of some forty persons, is divided into three sections: visits, ceremonials, and special services. Each is headed by an assistant chief of protocol under the administrative supervision of the chief of protocol. A deputy chief of protocol may absorb some of the administrative details owing to the demands on the protocol chief's time made by the White House and the Diplomatic corps.

The functions of the Office of Protocol include the organization and execution of activities bearing on the recognition of foreign ambassadors, ministers, charges, and consular officers. It maintains accreditation and other official records on all foreign Diplomatic representatives and their staffs. It maintains and publishes lists of those entitled to Diplomatic privileges including customs clearances, tax immunity, and others. It determines their *prima facie* eligibility for such rights, privileges, and immunities under United States or international law or treaty to which the United States is a party. It provides technical guidance in the negotiation of consular conventions and treaties involving the aforesaid Diplomatic rights, etc. It represents the Department of State in the handling of complaints or incidents involving foreign government representatives. It plans and provides escort for the visits and itineraries of foreign heads of state and heads of government, and prepares the official functions of the secretary of state. It obtains clearances for foreign government naval vessels requesting permission to visit United States ports, and for foreign military overflights and landings on United States territory. It also serves as the official clearance channel for United States vessels seeking to touch at foreign ports. As mentioned earlier, it provides assistance to some 120 Diplomatic missions in Washington with respect to orientation, travel, schooling, housing, and other matters. It maintains records of awards, gifts, and decorations conferred on United States officials by foreign governments, and drafts and defends legislation concerning the handling of such gifts and decorations. Protocol is the official source of advice concerning precedence, titles, invitations, flags, dress, and official funerals. Entries in my daily appointments book remind me that Protocol was not a haven for lethargy.

According to our records, during the two years and a day that my wife and I served in Protocol, we attended some twelve hundred receptions and four hundred dinners. The experience viewed in that light alone would qualify as one to trade sight unseen for a cabin by Walden Pond or its latter-day equivalent by the Lake of the Ozarks. But the entertainment obligations constituted only the glittering tip of a challenging subsurface of problems and insights that we encountered by day. The diary of no single day or week reveals the whole spectrum, but the following days in May, 1966, give a glimpse of the coloring.

Thursday, May 5, 1966

9:15 A.M.—*Secretary's staff Meeting. Charlie Frankel, assistant secretary for cultural affairs, brought up the cases of two young Americans, one of whom attending the East-West University in Hawaii refused to pay any taxes because the money is spent on Vietnam, or so states. The other has taken the stars out of the American flag and replaced them with dollar signs. It is hoped that the university authorities will find reason to withdraw the federal grants. If they don't, according to William Crockett (deputy under secretary for administration), Congressman John Rooney will take care of it for them.*

10:30 A.M.—*The dean of the corps called. He gave his*

cumplimentos *on the Diplomatic reception at the White House, then said he wished a very informal approach to be made to Secretary Rusk concerning an invitation to President René Schick of Nicaragua to pay an official visit to the United States in late June or July. Sevilla said he wished to "fulfill his responsibility" to his own President—he said he mentioned the idea to President Johnson at the reception who seemed receptive and suggested he submit it to Rusk. He said he was spreading the word through the corps that I had taken an active interest in seeking protection for the embassies.*

11:45 A.M.—I arrived at Fort McNair for the luncheon in my honor given by General Herrick, commander of the Military District of Washington. There were a number of naval and military officers there. I met them all and spoke briefly—greetings and gratitude. Then, not staying to eat, I hurried off to the Diplomatic entrance at the White House just in time to meet the first ambassador for Jack Valenti's lunch, attended by the ambassadors of Sweden, Switzerland, Luxembourg, the Netherlands, Denmark, and Portugal. Valenti began in his usual way by pointing with pride at the President's accomplishments and embellishing these with personal notes of the President's stability in times of stress, recalling how steady he held his hand out for a glass of water on the plane back from Dallas. He seemed to want very much to counter the suggestion that the President is an impulsive or nervous man, one which none of the ambassadors had made. The President joined the group shortly afterward, spoke of his desire to secure a negotiated peace in Vietnam, which was, he said, "difficult." He said that many people in the world and here in our Congress, too, seemed to feel that the brown or Asian peoples were less important, "not our kind of people," therefore should be abandoned to whatever fate power in that area had in store for them. He, however, felt that their problems were our problems and that we should help. Only Ambassador Vasco Garin of Portugal had the fortitude to respond to the President and likened his situation in Mozambique and Angola to ours in Vietnam. Portugal was fighting the same kind of fight and Garin also hoped for early success in the Smith-Wilson talks on Rhodesia. It gave the President the opportunity to reply to the latter suggestion by saying that it was always better to talk than to fight and obviated the necessity of distinguishing between the presence of Portuguese colonial troops in Africa and our presence in Vietnam.

6:30 P.M.—I arrived at Congressman Hale Boggs' reception. The whole government was there.

7:30 P.M.—Sylvia and I attended the Iranian Embassy's reception for their Imperial Highnesses Prince and Princess Pahlavi.

Friday, May 6, 1966

8:00 A.M.—Dr. Kenrick checked the calf muscle—torn at tennis. It's okay. Must try not to limp around the President. Tennis has incapacitated his team— McNamara, Rostow, McPherson, Vance. He has threatened to abolish the sport.

11:15 A.M.—The Hungarian Chargé, Mr. János Radványi, called—a heavy, sorrowful, rumpled fellow. At first it seemed he had nothing particular to say. Then he remarked that the cold war really seemed to be over and it was time for the diplomats of the "bloc" countries to *mix more freely with Americans here in Washington. He also thought it would be helpful if the American trailing of Hungarian diplomats in New York was "less aggressive." He hated to use the word, he said. There were certain restrictions on Hungarian travel in the United States which were reciprocated purely pro forma in Hungary by putting the names of thirty cities in a hat and drawing ten, saying these would be restricted. Such restrictions would be removed when ours were. Since they had no missiles, there was nothing to hide. Of course, he said, the military in all countries like to be secretive.**

12:15 P.M.—I called on Ambassador Charles Lucet of France. I thanked him for the effort he made to attend the Diplomatic reception, cutting short a visit to Boston, and I apologized for the lateness of the invitations. He was very gracious and assured me there had been no difficulty. He had also been to Yale the week before and enjoyed the questions of the Political Union but told them at the outset that he would not discuss Vietnam.

I gave the Ambassador an outline of my ideas for the Diplomatic corps, including trips to small rural areas, entertainment for the Junior Diplomatic corps, and the establishment of a country club, with which suggestions he seemed in complete agreement. We discussed the situation of the African ambassadors here and Marxism in Africa. I mentioned the articles of Karl Marx and Friedrich Engels referring to the Slavs as "ethnic trash," and also

---

* Radványi, who later tearfully thanked me for being the first chief of protocol to visit his legation in twenty years, and boasted of the role Hungarian diplomats were playing in finding peace in Vietnam, eventually defected to the United States in the belief his own Government had duped him in this regard.

supporting American war on Mexico and the conquest of
Texas. The Ambassador said he was aware that Marx had
race prejudices.

1:00 P.M.—*Lunch at the Ghanaian Embassy with soon-
to-depart Ambassador Riberio, the Joseph Palmers,
Sylvia, Mr. Boafo, Counselor of Embassy, his wife, and
a charming cultural counselor, Miss Christian. Lunch was
not served until 2:00 p.m. It consisted mainly of peanut
soup, an orangy-tan colored soup with some chicken and
chicken fat in it and an oil slick on the top—highly
seasoned as well. Mrs. Boafo, who had enjoyed Australia,
was very disappointed by Moscow where she said everyone looked so sad. She had never tasted maple syrup,
which I am sending her.*

*During lunch Ambassador Miguel Augustus Riberio
turned to Sylvia and said it would not be necessary to
spend a long time on a visit to Africa since we had "already seen the zoo." At this he burst into laughter in
which no one joined.*

4:15 P.M.—*Conference with Ambassador Goldberg
concerning the protocol order of precedence applicable
to the secretary-general of the United Nations. Apparently U Thant feels, and Goldberg agrees, that he is
placed too far down the line behind all ambassadors to
Washington. We will study and see if he could not be
placed before or after the dean of the Diplomatic corps
as a quasi-Head of Government.*

5:00 P.M.—*I called on the British ambassador, Sir
Patrick Dean. He also endorsed my thoughts for the
corps and felt that most of the corps would not object to
the secretary-general taking precedence; the Latins, he
thought, might. The dean, he said, was a genial man, but*

suggested I get in touch with seven or eight key ambassadors to sound them out as I go along.

Monday, May 9, 1966

10:00 A.M.—*Staff meeting. Morale problems. How to move ideas at the White House.*

11:15 A.M.—*Courtesy call from Ambassador Alexander Matsas of Greece. We discussed the problems of writing poetry and drama; he was particularly concerned about the problem of revealing a character's innermost thoughts without unlikely monologues directed at the audience. This is one of the reasons he selected the deaf mute part for his* Croesus. *Matsas endorsed again the idea of frequent small trips for ambassadors.*

1:00 P.M.—*Lunch at Paul Young's with Dave Brody of B'nai B'rith Anti-Defamation League. Pleasant except for a Jewish hors d'oeuvre he insisted on and which neither of us could eat.*

3:00 P.M.—*Discussed chancery problems with Under Secretary Bill Crockett. Zoning, police, parking, crime.*

4:00 P.M.—*Received Ambassador Sukich Nimmanheminda of Thailand. He suggests I read the "San Kuo," ("Romance of the Three Kingdoms") if I wish to understand China.*

5:00 P.M.—*I left to pay a courtesy call on Ambassador Tan Sri Ong Yoke Lin of Malaysia. The White House driver got lost. Tried again at 6:00 p.m. and made it. The Ambassador served some rice cakes with cocoanut covering—good. We discussed Asia; he said that the Asian peoples were not anxious to be dominated by the Chinese and that those who oppose our policy in Vietnam both at home and abroad were mistaken. I asked him about Tibet, having in mind Senator Mike Mansfield's observation that the Chinese had ancient claims on Tibet based on centuries of subjugation and the relationship of Tibet as a tributary. Ambassador Ong echoed Ambassador Sukich Nimmanheminda of Thailand's recollection that this was not so—that, in fact, Tibet had been independent of China for centuries and had made incursions upon China from time to time. He also said that many people misinterpret as tribute gifts of minor consequence made from time to time by small nations to major nations in order to maintain cordial relations. He said on some occasions Chinese emissaries were beheaded in lieu of the gift.*

8:00 p.m.—Dinner at the New Zealand Embassy. A musicale with no bars held.

Monday, May 16, 1966

Morning—Swore in Foreign Service graduates, a wide-awake bunch. Pretty wives.

Afternoon—Drove with Sylvia to Oatlands in Leesburg and met with the Board of Trustees including Gordon Gray, head of the National Trust. A beautiful place which would need some expansion to accommodate state visits. A major problem for them would be keeping it open as a museum with the uncertainty of the visit schedule.

Evening—Dinner for Ambassador Henry Cabot Lodge at the White House. The President referred to Lodge as the leader of some quarter-million Americans in Vietnam. Lodge made no reference to the fighting there or those engaged in it, but did compliment the President for his courageous leadership. Mom and Dad there, Fulbright and Bob Hope, who said he had taken LSD Airlines from Berkeley to Harvard, and that everyone had his own movie.

Tuesday, May 17, 1966

9:00 A.M.—*Haircut with Assistant Chief of Protocol Sam King looking over barber's shoulder to explain the problem of King Faisal's wish to be met on the ellipse by the President, not at the White House.*

11:00 A.M.—*Swore in Findley Burns as ambassador to Jordan. Lunch at Sans Souci with Justice staff to discuss my final report of President's Committee on Juvenile Delinquency. I explained the meeting in the attorney general's office where the latter indicated a desire to keep the committee going quietly until next year, and retain the chairmanship. I also suggested that leadership should be devised to encourage county sheriffs and law officers over the country to expose themselves to expertise in the behavioral sciences and not to consider themselves the sole sources of knowledge concerning human conduct. As astute judge of human behavior, Art Buchwald, seated nearby with Ben Bradley, puffed dreamily on his noon cigar.*

3:00 P.M.—*John Tuthill, our ambassador-designate to Brazil, called with Jack Kubisch, Brazil desk officer. I recalled my efforts years back to meet the peasant leader, Francisco Juliao, thwarted by the embassy.*

4:00 P.M.—*James Habberton, executive director of the Business Council of International Understanding, called to request that state visitors be apprised of the interest of small groups of businessmen to entertain them at a dinner in the New York area. I suggested that if this was to further commercial purposes the idea might best come through the secretary of commerce to the President for feedback to us. I then asked if his group would be interested in assisting in the establishment of an international club. Not very.*

Tuesday, May 24, 1966

11:00 A.M.—*The ambassador from Burma called to discuss the Ne Win visit. Suggested schedule approved.*

2:50 P.M.—*Courtesy call on the Jamaican ambassador, Sir Neville Ashenheim. Discussed interest in fish flour and purchase of embassy house in northwest D. C. Asked about prejudice for future, very likely black ambassador. Also about the builders' integrity.*

3:50 P.M.—*Called on Ambassador Veljko Micunovic of Yugoslavia who took pains to indicate the difference in approach by the Yugoslavs and the Soviet Union on both cultural and economic controls. There were never restrictions on artistic or literary expression in Yugoslavia (no mention of Milovan Djilas) and the Yugoslavian government was trying to get out of the business of ordering the economy and was encouraging private initiative. There were, he said, some fifty private commercial agents in New York competing for American business. America, he said, was No. 1 in exports to Yugoslavia, and No. 3 in imports from Yugoslavia.*

5:15 P.M.—*Called on German Ambassador Henry Knappstein who took me on a tour of the embassy and indicated support of the concept of an international country club although he thought his staff was fairly well cared for in this respect. He personally likes to weekend at a cabin in Virginia.*

Evening—*A young woman telephoning for the Sheraton Hotels asked if I would care to join the "Dinner-a-*

*Month" club in order to get out and meet new friends. I
said I would think about it.*

Occasionally a chief of protocol does look up and discover he has free time. Normally at such moments he falls
asleep. But when it occurs at high noon, other alternatives compete for favor—a stroll, a hot dog with everything, girl-watching. An opportunity for creative effort
can even present itself. It did so for me one day in New
York during the momentary collapse of an Asian prime
minister.

Canceling all afternoon engagements from his Plaza
suite, I then called an old college friend who had secured
steadier employment than mine as a television writer
and producer. Sascha Burland was, and undoubtedly still
is, his name. As Whiffenpoofs at Yale we had serenaded
everything that moved and a few that couldn't. After
graduation, with a third former Whiffenpoof, Harry
Thayer, now a State Department China hand, we shared
a one-room flat on the West Side across the street from
a home for unwed mothers. With its cockroaches, old-
fashioned gas jets, which could not quite be turned off, a
landlady named Flo Dunk and her drummer son, Billy,
our place had a charm, which wore off only after Billy,
a dope addict, shot himself in the bathtub. We closed
out our bachelor days in the relative serenity of Green-
wich Village near Washington Square, where guitar
players were not yet being arrested. In the early 50's we
went our separate ways. I with a law degree back to St.
Louis, Sascha into the reserved embrace of an ad agency,
and our friend, Harry Thayer, into *Newsweek.* For a

while we kept in touch by exchanging by parcel post the old frying pan that had scorched our eggs.

Sascha was getting set to record a commercial when I called. I met him at the studio. The job at hand was a sound track for an Alka Seltzer TV spot. The film depicted a tired motorist with a nagging family and headache to match. A filling station attendant provides him with a bubbling Alka Seltzer. He smiles and drives off, oblivious to the continuing tantrums of his unpleasant children. As relief comes, a background of jarring music subsides into a gentle three-part whistle.

But the third whistler had not arrived. Costly studio time was wasting. Would I, the Chief of Protocol for the United States of America, provide the third whistle? Ask not! Alka Seltzer had done so much for me; I owed it to Alka Seltzer. Also, I carried the requisite union cards. It took ten minutes. The lead whistler was pleased. "Buddy," he said, "let me know if you ever need work."

It was a comforting thought for the tattered chief.

Occasional breaks in the routine provided the chance to think anew how the office could better perform the function of enhancing the context of state and official visits and other diplomatic encounters. One intriguing problem was finding an equally charming but closer alternative to Williamsburg as a historic watering hole for visitors to refresh their jet-jarred spirits before pushing on to Washington and the official welcome. Both New York and Philadelphia provided challenging competition, particularly the latter with its Independence Hall and the Liberty Bell. But each suffered two distinct

disadvantages: distance from the capital, and an over-
whelming municipal fervor to entertain the guest—precisely what we were trying to spare him from until his
biological clock was reset on local time. Williamsburg's
unhurried atmosphere, like its restored colonial houses,
conveys a sense of timeless peace, which may gently
beckon a curious sovereign to take a closer look but will
definitely accommodate a sleepy one.

Under the old-world guidance of its president, Carl
Humelsine, and his colleague, Duncan Cocke, Williamsburg is as tranquil a base camp before the final assault
on the summit as could be found. But the problem of
distance is not entirely disposed of. It requires a helicopter flight of an hour and five minutes to proceed from
the helipad on the Williamsburg golf course to the landing area by the Washington Monument.

Helicopters, even the President's, are not yet designed
or configured to provide elegant transportation. Add a
touch of weather, and between bumps and pleasantries
yelled over the roar of the rotors, one is led to wonder if
the peace of mind so lately won in the hills of Virginia
is not lost in the skies above them! I carry the indelible
memory of many an eerie smile of princely reassurance,
in answer to my shouted expressions of solicitude. And
suppose flight conditions should encourage or counsel a
visit to the "facilities"? These consist of a chemical
bucket-apparatus in the aft compartment past the curled
feet and impassive gazes of security guards and attendants. However sanitary they are, facile they are not. And
when the tiny door won't open and, once open, won't
close, and when closed, won't open, and the need is a
lady's, in a long robe that snags and a high coiffeur that
must carefully bow for admittance to a chamber devoid of

a washbasin and too low to permit standing, protocols fancy turns to more serviceable arrangements.

Among the many alternative suggestions were two that warranted examination. One of these was Mount Vernon, not the homestead shrine itself, but an appropriate residence built on the premises, out of sight of tourists, with its own separate access. The visitor would be close to Washington, and feel the sincerity of the welcome from the sacred soil itself. A special tour of George Washington's home and grounds would be afforded.

This idea was advanced by Betty Beale, the Washington columnist and a long-time friend. I visited Mount Vernon, spoke with the director, and left that pleasant experience with new information and sufficient discouragement. Mount Vernon is not owned by the United States Government. The Government early in the nineteenth century saw no reason to buy it even in order to save it from obliteration. But a lively group of ladies perceived what the Government did not. Organizing the Ladies' Mount Vernon Association, they bought the property and have held it to this day. They control its use, and no one can doubt they not only have performed a public service of inestimable value, but have done it well, dedicating the premises to the enlightenment and pleasure of unending generations. They are perhaps not unreasonably concerned over departures from normal usage—including the sumptuous dinner arranged for the Shah of Iran by Mrs. John F. Kennedy. I recall accounts of that evening, which seemed to bring needed luster and imagination to our diplomatic style. I am not familiar with any of the precise difficulties encountered. I only know that the sensitivities ruffled in 1961 had scarcely been smoothed by time and tragedy. And the idea that

Mount Vernon might provide a permanent site for diplomatic hospitality was clearly one that would have to await some changes in philosophy, which is to say, in philosophers.

Next in line for consideration was Annapolis. This possibility was brought to my attention by another group of ladies, comprising the Association for the Preservation of Historic Annapolis. These ladies saw the salvation of one of their dearest projects—the restoration of the old Paca House—in its designation as a stopover for state visitors. William Paca, a signatory of the Declaration of Independence and governor of Maryland from 1782–1795, was one of the few early American political leaders of Italian descent. His spacious home sits in the center of Annapolis, a block from the state capitol. The buildings of Annapolis, unlike Williamsburg, need not be rebuilt from scratch. They still stand. There is a historic authenticity to the place that few American towns can match. The facilities and history of the Naval Academy add a unique dimension to its relevance to the intended purpose. At the outset of the nation's history, it was a principal port of entry for newly designated ambassadors and other distinguished visitors on their way to Washington. By adopting it for this purpose, we would merely be reinstating an old custom. What was needed was money. I suggested the ladies contact the Italian-American community—Baltimore's Mayor Thomas J. D'Alesandro III, Jack Valenti, Frank Sinatra—and secure support for restoring a home and garden that were true Italian roots in colonial soil. One can imagine the verve with which some other ethnic groups might have approached the challenge. But the ladies, with Anglo-Saxon restraint, were slow to entreat, and the Italian Americans slow to respond. In any event, there was little or no progress made in my time.

During this period my attention was drawn to another silhouette on the Maryland horizon—the listing hull of the U.S.S. *Constellation,* first man-of-war to fly the American flag, whose keel was laid before that of her sister ship, the *Constitution,* and who served as our flagship in World War II. She was pictured in a Washington newspaper, a rotting hulk, lying untended off Baltimore. In that very issue was the story of a $12 million United States Government grant to assist Egypt in lifting the ancient and ponderous monument at Abu Simbel from its flood-threatened position to high ground. It was thus to be made safe from the spreading waters of the Aswan Dam, which had figured so prominently in the bankruptcy of the United States Mideast policy of the late 50's. It was said that $1 million would restore the *Constellation* to her fully rigged glory.

I dreamed of her lying in the Potomac in the sight of Washington, Jefferson, and the other Presidents she served. I thought of her receiving state visitors with our President as host. In her first major engagement she forced the French ship *Insurgente* to strike her colors. I pondered the scene of Johnson on her foredeck offering a vintage claret to de Gaulle. The old ship, present at our birth, was being allowed to die while we shored up the heirlooms of other nations. And I wrote:

> America would pace
> The million dollar race
> To lift a pharaoh's face

As if we need him,
While soberly we've shunned
To use a federal fund
To save a ship that gunned
The way to freedom.

So worldly we've grown
We're propping up a stone
Ordered from the throne
When men were chattel,
While screams the lonely gull
And weeds embrace the hull
That never knew a lull
In freedom's battle.

Unmastered and unmanned
She sinks in sight of land
Without a helping hand
Much less a prayer.
Let's take her out to sea,
And cut the lady free,
To don a wave and be
With men who care.

It wasn't a Holmesian success, in the class of "Aye, tear
her tattered ensign down," but it brought grateful letters
from a good many old Navy men. My suggestion that
she be brought to Washington, however, encountered
stout rejection from some Maryland legislators, one of
whom demanded that we keep our "Diplomatic mitts" off
the treasured relic. The day of this pronouncement, the
ship actually sank at her berth. From that time on, however, for whatever cause—fear of big possessive Government, guilty conscience, awakened patriotism—the ship

has enjoyed new attentions on her way to a permanent berth at Fort McHenry. If I helped start her down the slips to that immortal place, I'm proud indeed.

I never thought of the protocol job as more than it was, a chance to smooth the way for the great and occasionally the small. Delivering a pep talk to a hundred diplomats about to tour the states, I was frequently interrupted by an infant in the front row. With an efficient little motion she would fling her pacifier at my feet, and I would return it to her. This was faithfully reported in the press, and one of the nicest letters I ever got was from a lady who felt she "knew what my job must be like," and said it would be easier if I would only remember to "tie the pacifier to baby's neck." Good advice!

The two years in Protocol, which splashed my life with champagne, parades, colorful assemblies, and the sonorous rhetoric of peace, recede now in memory. The scenes fade into a kind of unreality from which, it seems, they came. Pressing more vividly on my mind are other scenes, other meetings, conducted without benefit of ruffles and flourishes but, somehow, less forgettable. To see, much less solve, the true needs and urgent problems of people requires piercing the velvet veil of protocol and the burlap veil of bureaucracy

PART TWO

PIERCING THE VEIL

CHAPTER ONE

The next best thing to agreement is courteous disagreement. Even anger can be courteous if it is not infected with hatred. Yet opposition without hatred is a necessary condition for peace, that state of equilibrium between what men or nations want and what they can be induced through reason or compassion to believe others could credibly claim for themselves. Hatred robs them of their capacity to be so induced. Worse, it robs them of compassion. If only love were as blind.

How does one come to an understanding of the part hatred or the conquest of it plays in the ordering of human affairs? More through example, I think, than precept. I learned it, among other things, from my father, a competitive man. In any argument or challenge, of minutes or months, he displays a solidity of determination that matches the jaw lines of Mount Rushmore. Yet familiar to his adversaries, in addition to his persistence, is his courtliness, his humor, and the uncanny absence of grudge regardless of the strain of the struggle or the outcome. These qualities are lashed to the mast, and will either go down with the ship or ride out the storm.

It is unfortunate that a father's life cannot be rerun before the eyes of a grown son who missed the first show during his oblivious childhood. Too many boys grow to manhood without knowing the challenges their fathers faced. And not knowing their fathers' challenges, they do not know their fathers. Such knowledge takes time and luck.

In growing up I saw my own father as a kind of Titan, or demi-god, moving irresistibly upward and onward. Company presidencies and government secretaryships came naturally to him. Cover stories in *Life* and *Time* seemed natural forms of recognition. Away at school and college, I found my father's honors comforting but remote. His confrontations with some of the less selfless cronies of President Truman, the fight for a separate Air Force, defense of the B-36 (which interrupted the first and only family trip we had ever planned), the mobilization problems of the Korean War, and his "goldfish bowl" administration of the Reconstruction Finance Corporation, six successive unanimous confirmations by the Senate he would one day join—such matters would rise and fall like moderately heavy waters before the prow of a proud ship.

It was not until his first race for the Senate in 1952, when he asked for my help, and my brother's, that he suddenly came into focus for me as a natural man—not an ordinary man, to be sure, but a mortal one at least. For him the transition from boardroom to hustings was abrupt and demanding. In that hottest of summers we drove some twenty thousand miles together as a family throughout the state of Missouri. We came to know the agonies as well as the satisfactions that cram a candidate's album of memory. My brother and I discovered what our mother doubtless already knew—that it was possible for our father to become grim, to make mistakes,

to misspeak himself, to suffer reverses. We began thinking of him in a new way—because to an extent, he
needed us. To discover that possibility, in my case at the
age of twenty-four, was a curious sensation, unsettling
yet strengthening. Aside from rare illnesses, I had never
been solicitous about my father. He was the one individual who could take care of himself. Now, beleaguered by
predictions, first of primary defeat by Mr. Truman's hand-
picked candidate, second of being swept away in an
Eisenhower landslide, he walked unwavering into the
contest. I see him standing in a rumpled seersucker suit,
hair blowing in the hot summer wind, on a hundred
courthouse lawns; jumping out of the car to visit an
isolated farmhouse; bending the ear of an elderly country
newspaper publisher behind the clutter of a roll-top desk
while among drowsing cats a grease-covered boy worked
the press.

The inevitable political charges of past errors were
made in full measure by my father's two opponents, one
of whom, as an incumbent Senator, had written him a
letter upon his resignation from Government, in unstint-
ing praise of his public service.

It would be inaccurate to say my father maintained an
even temper during this period, in spite of the guiding
steadiness of his great and close Missouri friends, former
Governor Forrest Smith, Judge Ernest Tipton, Jim Meredith, Stanley Fike, Sid Salomon, Clark Clifford, and others.
But even in the most desperate moments when we had
all run out of comforting things to suggest, he would not,
or perhaps could not, reply in kind. Any thought that this
Jobian forbearance was mere dogged political strategy
was dispelled two years later when he went out

again to meet an adversary he, like many other senators, could have avoided.

This adversary posed no immediate threat to my father's political position. He merely threatened the country. He did so by his implication in both substance and tone that half of it was traitorous. The threat was deadlier in that, as my father perceived, it was believed by many to benefit the land. Senator Joseph McCarthy himself certainly entertained the thought that his investigations in substance and style were good for the country. At least he saw no great harm in them. According to William J. Evjue, the aging publisher I met in Madison, Wisconsin, during the 1960 campaign, McCarthy "got" the communist issue while lunching with two priests. He had asked them, "What would be a good issue at this time?" Later, said Evjue, they rued their advice.

But once unleashed in that aura of Korean stalemate, of iron curtain intransigence, of lost freedoms in East Europe—in short, of a growing communist conspiracy with "agents and sympathizers" in the United States—it did not seem prudent to challenge McCarthy's clarion cries. This was the apparent judgment of the incumbent President, and at least three future contenders, a "silent majority" as it were of Presidential hopefuls, in addition to certain stalwarts of the Senate and House.

But when I first saw my father with Senator Joe McCarthy, I felt that somehow they were on a collision course. It was a hearing in New York, in 1953. The circus had come to the big top. I went downtown from Columbia Law School to see it. Reed Harris, author of *King Football*, in his undergraduate days at Columbia, was defending his record with the USIA. McCarthy went for him with an easy, cynical assurance. It was his special format, not in the orderly spirit of inquiry, but a kind of good-natured, rollicking inquisition, played to the gallery. Harris acquitted himself well. It put McCarthy in a bad mood. But he offered a ride for us all back uptown, my father and I in the back seat, with the columnist Leonard Lyons, and Lyons' young son, not over twelve, in front between the driver and Joe. Draping his arm along the seatback, McCarthy spoke abusively to the driver in language unfit to be spoken in the presence of a child. But it seemed to relax the chairman; he laughed and winked at us, oblivious to the boy. We sat in stony silence. The ride was too long. The moments ticked like the first snowflakes of an impending winter. And winter came. It lasted well into spring when McCarthy's challenge to the integrity of the Army polarized him from at least one senator, Stuart Symington.

As a member of a subcommittee that McCarthy chaired, my father had already displayed—without rancor or contentiousness—his concern for the victims of the unceasing scythe. When an elderly black woman, Mrs. Annie Lee Moss, was called to account by McCarthy for past, allegedly communist leanings, she denied the charge. While McCarthy looked on, bemused, Missouri's Junior Senator brought a hush to the hearing by saying quietly to Mrs. Moss, "I believe you. And if because of these proceedings you become unemployed, come see me. I will get you a job."

"History," wrote John Crosby, "turned a small but important corner" in that moment. My father never came back to that intersection for another look. He was on a straight road that led relentlessly to the televised contest with McCarthy at the crest of the latter's power.

It must be remembered that the Army–McCarthy hear-

ings placed in opposition a Republican senator and a
Republican Cabinet officer, Army Secretary Robert Stevens, appointed, of course, by the Republican President.
Accordingly, as the President stood aside, it was considered the better part of Democratic valor to do likewise,
at least until the Administration played its cards face up.
Nor had the role of the vice presidency been yet elevated
to that of national moral adviser. The silences of the President were not broken by the vice president.

In the meantime, what had been wistfully looked upon
as broad farce by responsible men had become a clear
threat—a juggernaut. Yet as luckless colleagues were
mowed down, reputations tarnished, careers ruined, most
"responsible" men had joined the silent two at the top,
hoping for the Wisconsin Senator to fall in a hole, yet
unwilling to be caught with a spade. They sensed what
my father articulated in a warning to Secretary Stevens
—that the Wisconsin Senator would not fight by the
Marquis of Queensbury rules.

But, as Michael Straight wrote in the *New Republic*
of June 21, 1954:

> Symington was neither judicious nor cautious; he was a par-
> ticipant by instinct, and bold—above all in this case. . . . Or-
> ganization Democrats were privately appalled at disclosure
> of his intervention in an internal Republican fight. They
> felt it obscured the Republican responsibilities, and deprived
> the Democrats of the full benefit of the dispute. But Syming-
> ton was not acting as a party man. To him Army morale and
> the Subcommittee Chairman were not party affairs. . . . In
> the drama he became what Stevens could not, and none other
> would become—the protagonist.

That had been, in a way, his life's role—for failing
companies, a separate Air Force, strong defense, efficiency

in business and government, and fairness. Under his stewardship the Air Force was the first service to implement President Truman's integration order. To defend Annie Lee Moss was natural. To defend the integrity of the military was visceral. And it cost much. In addition to the skepticism of the old pros, fringe detriments included obscene phone calls to my mother, threats, curses, and strong opposition to further political progress.

I had been married a year and was living in a West Side apartment while finishing law school. During the Army–McCarthy hearings the ten-block walk to the Columbia campus was an eerie experience. The usual bustle of morning sounds was missing. The only noise to be heard from the numberless windows of the tall buildings was the droning voice of Counsel Ray Jenkins, or McCarthy's nasal querulousness, or Stevens' injured indignation. The city was mesmerized. Something was happening to people. It was fear.

Our service at neighborhood grocers, tailors, and other stores improved measurably. "You any relation to the Senator?"

"He's my father."

"Good boy."

The silent majority at that time consisted, as it does today, of some who had read and understood enough of history to fear its repetition. When McCarthy put Roy Cohn on the stand, and asked him if he could understand Symington's position better if he knew he had "communist cronies," I knew he was closing the ring, and not one drawn by the Marquis of Queensbury. McCarthy himself cheerfully espoused the morality of "Injun Charlie" who would kick senseless any person approaching in an unfriendly manner.

I watched my father's expression. It reminded me of the composure of the Spartan general who, on hearing that the enemy were drawing nearer, remarked, "Good, then we shall be nearer to them." Cohn had no desire to be caught between hammer and anvil, and evaded the question. But McCarthy swung again, implying cowardice. My father answered:

"You said something about being afraid. I want you to know from the bottom of my heart that I'm not afraid of anything about you or anything you've got to say anytime, anyplace, anywhere."

There were few men in America who would have said that to Joe McCarthy at that time. There were none who had. It separated a man from a good many boys. It was followed by my father's characterization of McCarthy's files as the "sloppiest . . . in government," and the suggestion that McCarthy's own finances merited inspection. Still, these remarks were made in anger, not in hate.

At the conclusion of the hearings, few Americans still occupied themselves with the question, "Who promoted Perez?" (McCarthy's opening challenge). Most wondered, on the contrary, how such a quixotic figure as McCarthy's could bestride the nation for so long, and breathed relief to know the genie had been wrestled back into the bottle and turned over to the Watkins Committee for analysis. Lawyer Joseph Welch had a hand in it, as did Senator Ralph Flanders. But the man who held at Thermopylae, "in obedience to his country's laws"—and his own conscience—was Stuart Symington. Yet, as there was no bitterness on his part in the struggle, he took no particular pride in the outcome. Lesser participants, some journalists, and certain summer soldiers figuratively circled the city of Washington, dragging the body from their chariots. Former hovering backslappers hovered no more. Joe knew who they were. His desk seemed to have an invisible moat around it. And when, in his lonely isolation, he thought to phone a colleague for a roast chicken dinner, he called my father. When the tide of despair and illness closed over him, among the names listed on a resolution recognizing his better claims was my father's. Criticized by the curious kind of liberal opinion that despises generosity of mind, he replied that it did not seem appropriate to carry the struggle beyond the grave.

Early in my first campaign for Congress, I received an irate letter from a gentleman who asked me to consider if I had ever done anything in my life without my father's help. I recalled, in reply, George Washington's assertion that everything he was he owed to his father and mother.

"Me, too," I concluded.

CHAPTER TWO

"Not until we know the Russians better," was the answer. The question, put to the Defense Department spokesman was, "When can the arms race subside?" It was asked by one of the members of the Democratic Study Group at a breakfast meeting in the Rayburn building in the fall of 1969. The Study Group is a loosely organized collection of Democratic congressmen, with a small staff, and an evolving agenda focused on national and world problems that somehow have not yet captured the attention of the whole House. The Republicans have a similar organization, the Wednesday Club, which meets on Monday.

"We just don't know the Russians very well," sighed the speaker. It occurred to me that we just didn't know anyone "very well," including ourselves, and that if "just not knowing" was an automatic justification for building and deploying the next weapons system, the two great confronters will be so bowed over by the weight of our respective "survival packs," we won't be able to look up and shake hands when we reach the top of escalation hill. We can simply topple forward and exchange gifts. The tools of "diplomacy" are no longer the pen and the sword alone. Add the spade. For diplomacy today is the art of digging for common denominators in human aspiration, and building the foundations of peace upon that kind of rock. The presence of differences, in social, political, or economic philosophy cannot be allowed to obscure the commonality, much less postpone the search. Surely there is enough in Russian literature, drama, and the arts to reflect a commitment to the human spirit. The wrenching, distorting experience of revolution, despotism, and harsh censorship has clearly injured and offended the spirit. But who could have so little faith in human nature as to believe they could kill it?

A certain hardening of the arteries of sentiment is observable in many of the men who have climbed the slippery pole to power in the Soviet Union. But it is unrealistic to think that they, so especially experienced in survival techniques, would be engaged in an uninterrupted plot to atomize the United States and all its friends and bases. To reign over ruin could be the ambition of no sane man. Territories made barren by atomic warfare are not an inviting prospect for the conqueror: no timorous girls with flowers, no flowers, no burgeoning fields or men to till them. The nuclear no-man's land, not only biologically, but psychologically uninhabitable, could only darken, giving off vapors of eternal reproach to the men and nation that unleashed such inhumanity.

If those whom the gods would destroy they first make mad, when does the madness set in? At the point of release of the holocaust? No, clearly the madness begins and consists in confusing the power to devastate with the power to converse. In other ages of man, a brief could be made for the suggestion. These were ages when man's cruelty to his kind was the rule, when defenses against aggression, both moral and military, were rather feeble, and the consequence horrifying but localized—a squiggle on the seismograph of history. Today in the era of instant communication, there is new awareness, and concern for minimal treatment of one another, often breached, but seldom without notice or with sanction. We've carried our old wounds, ethnic and national, a long way down the trail. Many of us owe our survival to a military capability that has kept pace with the challenges. No one could argue a unilateral farewell to arms; yet the nuclear powers, long eyeing one another, now glance nervously at the kibitzers who would like to get in the game and well may as short cuts are developed to detonate H-bombs. Intact, mankind has crossed thresholds of threat, battle, and war. We are now at the threshold of Armageddon. Here we should pause, and before investing in the next generation of weapons, think of the next generation of humans. What does the arms race mean for the human race?

Like most Americans who grew up with the atom, I worried very little about its power until we were obliged to share it with that "puzzle wrapped in an enigma," Russia. Our society had grown to accept the iron curtain with the calm of the Truman era. The giant geniality of Alben Barkley, Chief Justice Fred Vinson, and Speaker Sam Rayburn, the witty sallies of Clark Clifford and other friends of my father provided a backdrop of pleasant stability. I used to sing and strum a guitar for my share of supper at these languid, old-world laugh-ins. Only my father seemed to play the role of Cassandra, dwelling on the imminence of a Soviet atomic capability or urging bemused statesmen to secure European arrangements with Stalin before that time. Then, in the winter of 1949, after the September explosion of the first Soviet A-bomb, the horizon darkened. The temporary euphoria of nuclear monopoly faded. It was a new game, or, what was sadder, the old game with new stakes. The earlier defeat of the Baruch plan, the implacable visage of Stalin, the spy exposures, all combined to make me doubt that Lady Luck had the inventiveness to see us through. Assigned a sonnet in English class at Yale I wrote,

STONE AGE REVISITED

A sombre dawn reveals the crusted plow
For centuries transfixed and long since blown
With plowman's dust; another age of stone
Is born. The suppliant elm is rigid now.
Awakening airs caress the reaching bough
In vain, and weep, these winds, for they alone
Have breached the dim abyss between the known
And the unknown to kiss the greying brow
Of Earth, and grieve within the broken tower
At the lost inheritance, the final stand,
The crawling in the streets, the desperate hour,
When anguished curling of an outstretched hand,
In mute defiance of an ebbing power,
Scratched, "We cannot die," upon the sand.

I showed it to my father. His response: "How are you doing in your math?" In those days he feared, not without cause, that a streak of romanticism might numb my reflex responses to the demands of the technological age. He was a pragmatist with foresight. It was the foresight of a fertile mind, hospitable to alternatives, but firm in final decisions.

Earlier, in the winter of 1946, my brother and I sat on the edges of our chairs in his study one evening and listened to him. Noninterrupting listening calmed him and, from our point of view, he was at his best, calm. Brother Tim (Stuart, Jr.) had emerged at twenty-one a corporal after Army adventures in both theaters of the war. At nineteen, I was a recently discharged Marine private.

"What will you boys be studying when you get to Yale?" was the paternal question put with that familiar intensity which had long led us to realize he had a better answer than we did. After the usual pleasantries over such mythical courses as Early Roman Band Instruments, we came around to languages. "French, maybe, Spanish."

"I think you boys should take Russian," said the newly appointed assistant secretary of war for air. "In twenty-five years," he said, "we will either be fighting them or doing business. In either event we had better be able to talk." At this writing we are closing out the twenty-fifth year, and the prediction appears not to have been too fanciful. My brother took the advice in a timely fashion, and now speaks Russian well. Preferring to idle my way through the familiar arbors of the Western World, I delayed until my first year of law practice. The Korean War had come and not quite gone, and pessimists were considering Chinese. Still an optimist, I studied Russian with a series of patient people, principally Madame Gogotsky, a stimulating and attractive woman who had come in the 30's to dance for Sol Hurok and decided to stay for herself. Married to the talented Director of the St. Louis Institute of Music, she worked with me first at Berlitz and then on her own time. She enjoyed translating familiar American and English folk songs into idiomatic Russian, which was to be of great help to me.

There were other new St. Louisans from Russia. One family recalled the arrival of German troops in their independence-inclined Ukraine—"We met them with flowers." They recounted the needless brutality of Nazi occupation, and the resultant rueful determination that "if there is to be tyranny, let it be our own." Nevertheless, at war's end they sought and somehow found their several ways into the American-occupied zone of Germany. Now, reunited in America, they boasted a home, self-sufficiency, and a pretty daughter with a high school degree, "and no trace of accent, do you think?" The leisurely evenings of vodka, caviar, piroshki—a kind of pastry containing a hint of hamburger—and *narodni pyesni*, "folk songs," which my wife and I shared with them, filled me with a kind of bittersweet desire to keep them in this happy state.

I wondered if the people they left behind could be so different. I had to see the imprint of Stalin to believe it, and made plans to do so in the summer of 1957. The American Bar Association was to meet in London. I signed up in the hope of traveling on to Moscow for the Youth Festival. The State Department's nervousness about youth festivals abroad has become infectious. We have it at home now. Still, I had to balance my Walter Mitty fantasy of moving the world five paces to peace from a soap box in Red Square against such unknowns as the effect of such a display on the equanimity of Missouri's junior senator from whence came my help. I was dissuaded, but for only one year. Our brief stay in England, together with embassy changes, occasioned the invitation to return to serve as special assistant to Ambassador John Hay Whitney the following summer.

The State Department, already committed to a thorough probe of my background, and undoubtedly trying to sort out fact and fiction from the hilarious characteriza-

tions offered by my friends to sober-faced security men,
had to contend with my own additional request to visit
the Soviet Union before appearing officially en poste.

In the meantime, I discovered a travel agent who was
already arranging a Soviet visit for the chancellor of
Washington University, Ethan Shepley, his family, and
friends. I cast my lot with them. We were due to fly to
Helsinki in mid-July, and I stopped in Washington on
the Fourth. My father surveyed his prodigal and decided
to call the Soviet Embassy for the purpose of alerting
them of my plans, and possibly arousing some sympathy.
After all, how was he to know I had no intention to steal
bear statues from public parks, or deface the walls of the
Kremlin? The ambassador was away, but the minister,
Sergei Striganov, was willing to receive us. So it was
that I spent the afternoon of the Fourth of July, 1958, in
the drawing room of the Soviet Embassy, waiting the first
thirty minutes alone with the Senator engaging in the
kind of conversation that we thought might be monitored.
The Minister then strode in, ebullient, hospitable. We
discussed then recent grid-iron dinner, golf, folk music,
and peace. "He's a little younger than we are," said the
Senator; "maybe he can work it out."

"He will have a chance," said the Minister. I flew to
London, then to Helsinki, and on to Leningrad.

With my St. Louis friends, Mrs. Gogotsky's songs, and
a guitar wrapped in a wash-and-wear shirt, I flew first to
Helsinki where we learned that Marines had just landed
in Lebanon pursuant to an invitation not all the Lebanese
had signed. Champagne allayed our apprehensions and
we flew on to Leningrad where few of the people we met
had heard of Lebanon or could place it on the map—in
spite of their total immersion in strident radio and press

attacks on Amerikanski Aggression. In the streets and parks of Leningrad, Moscow, and Kiev the people were friendly, gentle, solicitous. I wandered for the most part unobserved or at least uninterrupted through various parks singing for children and then meeting their parents and other strollers. Their curiosity ranged from the man-hours of work necessary to buy a pair of shoes or a suit, to whether American wives all worked, to *Amerika Hochet Voenoo?* "America wants war?" asked with a kind of injured innocence. I hope and believe I answered the questions accurately, especially the last. The sessions were long and tiring. Beginning around 5 P.M. they would end around midnight when an old woman wearing a babushka or a young man with tousled hair would say, "He must rest now," and all would see me back to the hotel.

I was told by Intourist not to expect invitations to private apartments, but one group of teenagers did give me such an opportunity. Wedged between two iron bed-steads in an otherwise unfurnished room, we discussed the important personalities of the day: Dave Brubeck, Frank Sinatra, and durable old Bing Crosby. Dust-covered volumes of Lenin looked silently on from the wall shelves, as we talked and sang far into the night.

On another occasion I joined a group of men examining an American car. The Intourist guide told me in English to move away, we were "blocking the street." I translated the message to the crowd. "We stay," said one fellow. "It is our street."

I have warm memories of such meetings, of course, and chilly ones about other aspects of the visit, which expressed the distrust of the Soviet Government of its own people. Toward the end of my stay, minor officials began to wish to structure my impromptu sing-ins in a more organized way. Random camaraderie was not encouraged. Yet the Soviets know it is the key to the American heart.

How this key can be abused as well as used was illustrated for me in 1962 when as Attorney General Robert Kennedy's administrative assistant I met a bouncy attaché of the Russian Embassy named Georgi Borshakov. He was "Georgi" to everyone and he seemed to find satisfaction in being kidded. With self-deprecating nods, smiles, and circus English he enjoyed Bob's predilection for harmless buffoons, and had almost unlimited access to the inner sanctum of that office. This continued during the Cuban missile crisis. Ambassador Dobrynin also made frequent calls. Premier Khrushchev's account of these visits is incomplete at best—lacking any mention of Georgi, a known intelligence officer. I spent more time with Dobrynin in the attorney general's private elevator in one two-week period than later in two years of Protocol. In the cramped elevator we talked of music and Black Sea resorts, while in the office the talks were of a different character, presumably replete with mutual reassurances of good faith. But a good bye to Dobrynin at the elevator exit was often followed by a hello to Georgi at the front office. Whether these visits were coordinated or whether Georgi presumed to convey more reliable intelligence than the Ambassador was permitted to know, I must leave to files that I've never seen and perhaps don't exist. I did come to suspect Georgi's whimsical entree into the aorta of American decision at that time. The Soviets frequently convey their intent through unlikely and unofficial channels.

It was a difficult time for us all. I was given a desk and

phone at the Pentagon. The cables, the conjecture, and the anxiety and bluster of public figures from the Potomac to the Don did little to stiffen my confidence in the processes involved. One night I wrote out complete instructions to my family in the event of a missile attack during a period of separation. There were so many alternatives to consider that I ended up laughing. I finally wrote, "Head South—less industry—and warmer," named a few checkpoints, bought knapsacks at a surplus store, and found acquaintances doing the same. "Going camping?" I asked one.

"I hope not," he replied.

I packed the knapsacks carefully and hung them for quick grabbing in the basement. When the Soviet ships testing our Cuban blockade finally veered off, President Kennedy expressed his own relief by the precedent-settling handout of a gold memento to each participant in his key decisions. I gave out one concentrated protein cookie to each member of my family.

I remember no time in my life when the gap between communication and the anxieties such communication was intended to allay was greater. It was for this reason that I particularly resented Georgi's insinuating jocularity. The Attorney General undoubtedly suspected that Georgi was assigned to take advantage of his hospitality, and could have been one step ahead of him all the way. I do recall the reaction of John McCone, CIA director, to Bob's suggestion that Georgi join a group one evening aboard the President's yacht. McCone indicated that if Georgi went he would not. And Georgi, like the missiles, went back to Russia when the crisis passed.

Those were dangerous games, but Robert Kennedy played all the dangerous games, none of them without luminous courage, and most of them, God knows, well. Perhaps in the last analysis it was only with the complicity of Providence that we were able to assume a posture of credible deterrence. A break in the weather and the unanswerable indictment of air photography did the job. Clear skies over Cuba cleared the air in Washington. How Russia should look at Providence with our missiles at her doorsteps I leave to the Orthodox Church.

Providence itself was the subject of a discussion I had during the next Administration, but before Protocol was a bar for me to searching conversation. I had met a Soviet diplomat at a reception and invited him to lunch. I wanted to ask him some questions, and he clearly had plenty for me. I was interested in Soviet attitudes toward literary and theatrical freedom of expression. He wanted to know what kind of men were Bill Moyers, Jack Valenti, and others of the Johnson staff. Our responses were mutually uninformative. He also wondered, looking about the dimly lit room, overhung with cocoanut husks, nets, and dugout canoes, if Trader Vic's was a good place to meet girls. I told him it was more of a family restaurant.

After a couple of Navy grogs, he said very simply to me, "Jim, do you believe in God?" When I answered in the affirmative, he asked, "Why do you believe?"

I asked him to consider an unlikely hypothetical situation, the best I could summon at 2 P.M. on top of an Indonesian lamb roast with snow peas. I asked him to picture himself on the open sea in one of those frail dugouts leaking fast, with a sick stranger, unconscious, beside him. In the distance looms a ship. "You know your craft will sink before you are seen," I told him, "unless one of you leaves it. You are a great citizen, scientist, or what have you, with much to offer your country. All you know of the stranger is that he is a wanderer, a poet, a man who cannot compare with you in service to the state. Since he is unconscious, your decision is entirely your own. One must go that the other may be saved. What would you do?"

"I would go, and leave the other to be saved," said the Russian.

"Why?" I asked.

He paused. "Jim," he said, "do you not think I have capacity to love my fellow-man? I don't need God to tell me what I must do."

"He told you when He made you," I replied. "You're divine and don't know it."

The two theologians celebrated this impasse with cups of black coffee, and stumbled out into the glare of a day. I still look forward to learning to play the balalaika he sent the following week. Proving the nonexistence of God seems a preoccupation with the Soviet. There is no greater threat to the State than a doubting atheist.

One afternoon in the autumn of 1967, I met the poet Yevgeny Yevtushenko at my neighbor Art Buchwald's house. He spread his lanky frame comfortably across the sofa and invited questions. "What have your fellow authors Yuli Daniel and Andrei Sinyavsky done to warrant imprisonment?" I asked.

"They fouled their nest," said the young poet, whose own works have had varying effects on the nest. "I publish at home," he said. "They should not publish abroad."

"Would they have been permitted to publish the works in question at home?" I asked.

"No," he replied.

I asked him if he didn't think any man's view of the truth too important to be forcibly confined and suppressed, and if it shouldn't be free to surface somewhere in the world, if not everywhere.

"Perhaps," said Yevtushenko. "It is a good question." Then, donning his slouch cap, and swinging his wool scarf around his neck, he joined us in a game of touch football. After a wobbly pass, he would hold the pose for imaginary photographers, like any American boy.

Later, over a glass of wine he handed a book of poems to my wife, inscribed, "To Sylvia with secret love." I smiled with the self-assurance of a minor poet.

Do we "know the Russians better," I wonder, one hundred years after the day, November 20, 1871, when the Grand Duke Alexis, Czar Alexander's son, arrived at Sandy Hook aboard the prophetically named frigate *Svetlana*? Young Alexis, the guest of President Grant in gratitude for the earlier solicitude for the Union of his father, the Czar, traveled three months in this country, in the most extraordinary visit of this kind in our history —certainly an enviable one. From the parlors of Boston among the nation's leading literary figures, Lowell, Holmes, and Whittier, he entrained to Nebraska where he buffalo-hunted with General Sheridan, Custer, and Buffalo Bill a century too soon for TV coverage.

It was eight years earlier—1863—that a Russian fleet had steamed into New York harbor as a warning to the fleets of Victoria and Bonaparte not to intercede on behalf of the Confederacy. The officers and men were feted with a grand ball and a *soirée russe* at the New York Academy of Music.

"We know precisely," intoned *Harper's Weekly* in its issue of October 17, 1863, "what a foreign alliance might involve. Furthermore, we are no longer isolated from the rest of the world. Our commerce and our steadily increasing communication with all parts of the world, have made us a part and parcel of the great civilized community of mankind; nothing which happens anywhere is of indifference to us, and our transactions interest all the rest of the world."

"We all dislike," the editorial went on, "to see a principle of policy settled by the Father of the Country being brought into question; but still it is obvious that the world has kept on moving since Washington's time . . . an alliance between Russia and the United States at the present time would probably relieve both of us from all apprehensions of foreign interference . . . it would probably be the best guarantee against war."

Over a century later, in August, 1969, the Washington *Star* editorialized, "Considering the kind of world we live in, who can doubt the possibility that there may yet come into being a Soviet-American alliance?"

It comes down to the suggestion that we "know" people well enough if they're on "our" side, and we do not if they're not.

CHAPTER THREE

In 1961, I toured part of the hidden side of earth, the *barriadas* of Latin America. I wrote my wife on the back of a hotel menu in Lima,

If I were asked to look on the bright side of the sights we have seen, I would say that at least the people have not eaten their dogs yet—plenty of mangy little mongrels nuzzling the scrap heaps—people living in caves or mud shanties—no furniture—shredded clothes—filth. Yet they must be people. The little two-year-old cake of mud held up to me by her mother turned away . . . that little piece of mud was shy, so it must have been human. It's the same story—just new chapters—Caracas, Bogotá, Quito, Lima. As Venezuela's President Rómulo Betancourt told me at a four-course lunch yesterday, *El hambre no es un buen consejero,* "Hunger is not a good adviser."

I could see, on my Food for Peace mission to Latin America a decade ago, that a good many thousands were getting that kind of advice. They still get it. We have met millions whose counselor is hunger, in India, Asia, Africa, and the Americas, including our America. The signal characteristic of the 60's was our welling confidence that, avoiding the indecision of Hamlet, we would in fact "take arms against a sea of troubles, and, by opposing, end them." With Frank Sinatra's "High Hopes" as our theme, we came into the decade singing. We have left it sadder, wiser, but undefeated. We have lost skirmishes against poverty, but not the war. We at least have had the courage to look at the world's wounds. Only in attempting to dress them did we learn how deep they were. Where surgery was needed we had only poultices. Even that was a useful discovery. As a delegate to the United Nations Food and Agriculture meeting in Rome in October, 1961, I heard a Brazilian spokesman claim that the answer to hunger was not food but industrial development. I answered that in the meantime food might help. "Do nothing," said a returning American professor in my office that year, "nothing to reduce the death rate in Brazil"— a kind of passive final solution. "President Kennedy," I replied, "did not seek or win election on a promise to maintain death rates." Yet the view persisted that the only factor that could stabilize the food–population ratio was a high mortality rate, particularly among children. Quinine, sulfanilamide, and penicillin had disturbed the ratio enough, it was argued. At least let starvation perform its balancing function.

With these strange counsels echoing in my mind I visited many a starving community and discovered one phenomenon common to all: no one wanted to leave. Parents particularly had an aversion to seeing their children die. Any policy, it seemed, calculated to maintain the death rate in a given area of the world, would very likely encounter opposition from the people affected. And this was before the so-called "green revolution" in seed, fertilizer, and modern farming methods, which would bring many a famine-stricken land to the threshold of self-sufficiency. So the only difference between life and death for millions in the 60's was our ever-normal (which is to say, ever-loaded) granary. Nor were the political consequences of sharing the contents regrettable.

In his engaging book, *For Victory in the Peaceful Competition with Capitalism*, former Premier Khrushchev claimed the "capitalist nag" would never drag its chariot to victory over the Communist horse. Perhaps he had forgotten an old Russian proverb, "It is not the horse that pulls the cart; it is the grain." He had the proverb; we had the grain. It merely remained for us to determine whether we would consider our surpluses a problem or an opportunity. Senator Hubert Humphrey, originator of the idea of Food for Peace, had long since adopted the latter interpretation. President Kennedy saw that it caught the conscience of the American people, gave it his full endorsement, and appointed George McGovern, now Senator, as its director. As McGovern's deputy I spent months trying to initiate school-lunch programs in Latin America. Fourteen million United States youngsters were enjoying free or low-cost meals in school, so it was not a shameful or patronizing concept. Most of my reports were on the somber side, detailing conditions mentioned in the above letter to my wife. Yet sometimes I encountered a kind of happiness and contentment among the seemingly neediest beneficiaries of our earnest efforts, frenetic trips, and all-night conferences. I wondered at such times if we didn't appear a little foolish, not to say presumptuous, in our sudden breathless challenge to the passive patience of centuries.

There was certainly an amusing side to our rediscovery of the lost continent of South America. It occurred to me in the village of Puno in the high plains of Peru where with Under Secretary of State Chester Bowles, and others, we had just inaugurated a school-lunch program for thirty thousand children. To a friend I wrote the following irreverent account of that historic visitation by gringo eminences.

This place is 13,000 feet up. Everyone was fainting except the Indians. And they weren't paying much attention either. They wear little bowler hats, and red capes. Their faces look cut from brown clay with about as much expression as you might expect from a fellow whose civilization was interrupted four centuries back. But then they got out their reed pipes and knocked out a little pentatonic ditty—as I strummed feebly on my guitar, gasping for air. They were drinking chicha, a fermented corn beverage. With that, who needs air? All you need is a place to lie down. And there's lots of room for that. Ground, they've got. But you couldn't raise a cactus on it. It's rock hard—covered with a green furze you couldn't dignify with the name grass. You couldn't scrape it off with a pen knife. The cattle are a bony bunch, either lying down or grazing knee deep in the waters of icy Lake Titicaca on weeds—and maybe a few slow fish, for all I know. Anyway, the kids are going to eat for a change, and this might start something.

I made a five-minute speech. It was in Spanish. But it had to be translated into Aymara and Quechua by a fiery little lady who spoke twenty minutes to my five. I'm glad to know I can condense my remarks that much.

Of course, we had to get out, somehow. It was too high for the attaché plane, so we took the *ferrocarril*—an old Ford with railroad wheels—and went jogging right down the single track to Arequipa, whipping around the bends. What if a train comes, asks I. Win a few, lose a few, says the driver in faultless Quechua. On the way, we got stopped and nearly arrested by a local police chief. The charge: refusing to have a beer with him. The Ugly Americans did it again. But you never know about that Indian beer—the Inca's revenge.

An interlude, prior to our departure, underlined how difficult it is to give rational assistance to a country whose own people have not yet met. Following the school lunch-ceremony, and after the others had flown back to Lima, Ambassador Jim Loeb and I went to dinner in the small local hotel. We were interrupted by an embassy aide who told us there were three "pretty rough-looking fellows" in a side room waiting to see us. The aide said that, of course, "it would not be necessary" for us to see them. I said, "Khrushchev would see them." Loeb said he wasn't sure he liked the comparison, but that we would see them. We downed our coffee and went in.

They were "rough-looking fellows," Peruvian Indians, covered with dust and grime. They were sitting in a semicircle around our escort, Prime Minister Pedro Bel-trán's personal assistant, who had the unfortunate name—in Indian country—of Ponce de León, with Castilian features to match. *Tenemos un plan*, "We have a plan," he said. "A five-year plan and," extending his arms, "a ten-year plan."

One of the Indians stood. "We are sick of your plans," he said. "We must have action." Ponce de León was disturbed by the remark, but more so by our arrival in time to overhear it. He shrugged and left the room.

Here I remembered a conversation with my friend George Lodge, who, as the Eisenhower-appointed assistant secretary of labor for international affairs, had not yet been replaced by the new administration. "Do anything you can," he had said, "to meet the working people of Latin America and leaders in the labor movement." There was too little time, he said, to assume our message of good will or good works can get through government channels. To these "people's representatives," then, we introduced ourselves.

"Well," said the Indian spokesman, "as representatives of the United States, why don't you give your help, the food, the tools, directly to us, instead of to the Government, which shares nothing?" We explained the difficulty of circumventing Government in dealing with the people of any nation.

They nodded. "But try to get it through to us," said the leader. "We are desperate men. Our families, our friends, are dying." I said that no speeches or reports of the success of our aid program to Peru would I believe if we did not hear personally from them that help had arrived. And if it did not reach them, I said, I would consider the effort a failure.

They nodded and filed slowly out of the room. As they passed, the two Peruvian soldiers flanking the doorway, spat simultaneously at each. The Indians ignored this.

Not hearing from them for weeks, I wrote Loeb for their names and addresses. He never sent them. Perhaps he couldn't get them. Career officers staffing an embassy are generally reluctant to encourage communication with dissident elements in the local society.

Two years later, as administrative assistant to Robert Kennedy, I helped carry out one of his initiatives, which was to encourage our embassies to meet the people, especially youth, identify leadership qualities, and become accessible to their spokesmen. Has the policy of youth awareness survived Kennedy's tenure as attorney general? Many initiatives were taken in those days to accommodate the President's brother. That they happened to be worthwhile and overdue initiatives was too often ignored when that unique page of American history was turned.

It is clear, in any case, that we understand those we support as imperfectly as those we oppose, and since our management of both efforts depends on our own shared insights, teamwork, and cooperation, it comes back to how well we know ourselves. Want of such knowledge can turn an idealist into a quitter or a mindless bureaucrat.

Judge Thurman Arnold once observed, "We are immersed in vice, crime, deceit, greed and hate, which, if allowed to persist, could even lead to bureaucracy." The much maligned bureaucrat is, indeed, often thought to symbolize the pinnacle of man's inhumanity to man, primarily because of the suspicion that, once entrenched, he ignores and neglects the ills his office exists to curb. It is an unfair generalization, but one which would have less currency if its victims would step out into the crowd now and then.

No federal appointee should serve in the field, or in Washington, for more than a year at a time without some unstructured exposure, a chance to learn what the American people think of the problems he faces and to take and try to answer their questions. One of my assignments in 1961 as deputy to George McGovern, director of Food for Peace, was to travel our own country to discuss and explain the program. I met with civic, farm, business, and religious organizations from coast to coast, and despite their respective biases found one thing common to them. They supported the Food for Peace program. They believed in the idea. Some of them had a kind of blind faith in it, in the rightness of it. Others perceived the pitfalls—waste, corruption, shipping, storage, infestation—but believed that perseverant administrators could overcome them. "What can *we* do, here?" many would ask. Write your congressmen, we said. Support the voluntary agencies. Form local committees of support. For a time, strong national support was generated through the establishment of a Food for Peace Advisory Commission, with a membership that included George Meany, Mrs. Franklin D. Roosevelt, Bishop James Pike, James Michener, Marian Anderson. But such people are generally overcommitted. Friendly to good causes, they join far more than they can keep up with. The job of work remains for the lesser known.

Stationed at Puno, Peru, during my visit, was a junior embassy officer, James Boren, from Texas. I talked with him about getting the folks back home more personally and consistently involved. Our discussion led to the Partners of the Alliance for Progress in the State Department, a program by which United States cities and towns could establish a partnership relation to a Latin American community, and which Jim Boren later headed.

To stimulate this kind of interest and involvement, I told of things we had seen and heard in places like Laeticia. Laeticia was the name of one of the *barriadas*, "slums," that ring Lima, Peru. Forced by acts of God and man to leave the barren countryside, an unsmiling people, descendants of a proud race, had come to the tableside of the capital city to take its crumbs. In makeshift huts of wood, discarded posters, and bits of tin siding, they made their homes on the bleak hillside overlooking the neat paddock and tables where the Army fed and trained its horses. It was a mile from the health ministry. During the administration of Prime Minister Beltrán, the minister of health had never visited it. There at the top of Mt. St. Cristobal were a small school and chapel, little blobs of blue and pink as viewed from the air-conditioned rooms of the Hotel Crillon.

"What are you doing here?" asked my host at dinner. I explained the object of President Kennedy's Food for Peace mission—to seek uses for United States agricultural surpluses in the economic development programs of food-deficient nations. "But why come here?" continued my host, a successful businessman. "We are a well-fed people."

I pointed out over his garden and pool and the roof-tops of many houses to the far hill, where boys were carrying water on their shoulders up the slopes. "I was there this morning," I said. "They told us they were hungry."

"Oh, those people," exclaimed my host. "They've lived like that for centuries. They are used to it. You mustn't discuss such things with them. It will make them restless."

I was back on the hill in the morning. We had a meeting with the mothers of the school-age children. Would they be interested, we asked, in helping prepare and serve a school lunch? They were. Since the children did not eat at home, it would be good to have a meal at school. There would also be less begging and theft.

Within a few days we were providing bulgar wheat, which can be cooked like rice, and powdered milk in large cylindrical cardboard cartons, which were later halved into cradles. The "mothers' committee" came up with some vegetables. They boiled the water, as we had suggested, before reconstituting the milk. The youngsters lined up, clinked their new tin cups, and for the first time in their lives had food in school. It is good to see a child meeting milk.

The fathers then asked to see us. They said they thought the school was too old and dirty for children who could now eat there. They had decided to build another. They would tax themselves a few cents a month—every family—to buy the cement, and they would build during their free time, Sundays, and religious holidays. The new school went up pretty fast. One of the major political parties heard of the effort and offered to finance the entire undertaking, if it were named for their leader. The fathers turned them down, saying this was to be *their* school. I returned in the fall, and found it completed. The mothers and fathers asked if I could be present at the dedication and serve as *padrino*, "godfather," at the marriage ceremonies afterward.

"You are married, surely," I said.

No, indeed, they were not. It was costly, and seemed unnecessary when so many of the children died so young.

"But now that the children can eat," they said, "they should also have dignity." I was proud to stand by each couple as they knelt for the priest's blessing, with hundreds of children happily looking on. Later we played guitars, sang, and drank wine together.

Something more than a school had been built. We were still strangers to one another, but less so. We saw with our own eyes that helping people does not necessarily weaken them. They saw with theirs that we felt that way. The minister of health accepted our invitation to the dedication ceremonies, and puffed heavily up the steep hill, hitching up the trousers of his blue suit so the cuffs wouldn't trail in the occasional rivulets of waste. Recovering his breath at the top, he gave an exuberant address promising the continued support of the Peruvian Government "which made the program possible." Quite true, because without its permission we could not have entered the country on a mission of this kind. Would that we could have worked directly with the Indians of the *alto planos* as well.

CHAPTER FOUR

Of course, with respect to our foreign aid efforts, we had to get the permission of our Government, too. This was true even of the President who ordered the policy. Between a Presidential policy and its fulfillment are many men who remain unconvinced. A Presidential ombudsman to trace, find, and clear the bureaucratic blockages that slow his programs is the kind of tempting solution offered by those who are not familiar with management problems. Soon an ombudsman to monitor ombudsmen would seem called for. The job of forwarding Presidential policy directives is that of the respective department heads he appoints. Unfortunately, too many of these, like bewildered pilgrims on a new shore, put themselves gratefully into the hands of the populace they were sent at least to rule, if not convert. Immigrants at the top, they slowly swivel in their new leather chairs listening in awe to the bureaucratic folklore of that promised land. Their instruction will come from one or more timeserving beneficiaries of the status quo, who, "sympathetic" to each new director and the "demands on his time," will be glad to insulate him from the unnecessary details of management. Nevertheless, if he can shake off the spell and make surprise calls on the half-hidden offices of departmental subdirectors, he can have an enlivening effect on other personnel who have come to feel very remote, and therefore protected, from the Presidents they serve. Some have lifelines cast from the Congress. That is a complication. Congressional sympathy and cooperation with new ventures are difficult enough, unbeset by reports that old and faithful friends in the interested agencies are in jeopardy. This points up the need for a President to take the time, personally, to visit informally with key congressmen, not to trade pleasantries but to explain and persuade. The liveliest deputies, riding the Hill with carrots and sticks, are poor substitutes for the man himself. Of course, to do the job, the man must be informed. Congressional leaders, especially in food and agriculture matters, usually are.

Moreover, congressional attitudes are generally impervious to purely ceremonial attentions. For a committee chairman who has seen Presidents come and go, invitations to dine at the White House or fly to Mexico are pleasant and expected—but not per se calculated to move him. But economic self-interest, so often a bar to progressive thinking can also prove a stimulant to it. At one of the intersections of food and foreign policy, this is apparent.

In 1961, after addressing a Washington State Agricultural Association, I was asked to speak privately with some of its leaders. "Why is it," they asked, "that Canada can be selling half a billion dollars of wheat to Red China, and we cannot?" They then added, "Of course, if you say we asked, we'll deny it." They were interested in leadership initiatives, which would cut through the cant and mythology that enchained them, to achieve the sound business result that lay beyond. Yet there were at that time, and perhaps even now, men in positions of leadership, including some in Congress, who would support free food for Red China if she were starving, but wouldn't "trade" with "the devil." One can see the difficulty other nations have in dealing with this kind of schizophrenia. I was not a political figure, and my promise to convey directly the inquiry to the White House was all I could offer. Clearly, the logic of the point advanced by these conservative farm leaders nearly a decade ago was one that should have commended itself to their political leadership. There was the additional point that the conversion of scarce Red China foreign exchange into food prevented its investment in hardware. But I heard no more about it. We should bring these questions into the open when they occur, not in the reminiscenses of a generation that failed.

There has been many a slip 'twixt our cup and the lips of children of all the Americas, including our own. The larger foreign programs, such as those that virtually kept famine from overrunning India, Pakistan, and Indonesia, moved, under their own massive momentum, millions of tons a year, with the sanction of a Congress anxious to maintain subsidized agricultural prices and reassured that no "give away" was involved, since the law required payment in the currencies of the receiving nation. That such currencies, if not loaned back, were largely unusable, "frozen," was insufficient to shake congressional confidence in the program. With such hop, skip, and jump logic, we do some good things. With a more rational and consistent approach, we could do better. This would require introduction of honest assessments of progress

toward clearly defined goals. Even the vigor of Presidential mandates, if not continually refreshed, dissipates
quickly.

George McGovern, whom President Kennedy had
appointed director of Food for Peace, knew this. That is
why he, after walking the streets of Washington in search
of an office, settled on the idea of securing quarters in
the Executive Office Building next to the White House.
I am convinced that had he not done so, we would never
have been heard of. As it was, though privileged to
buttress our telephone messages with the reminder, "It's
the White House calling," within a few months' time we
would get the response, "*Who* in the White House is
calling?" After that we knew we were shortly to join the
ranks of the extinct. We would be snuffed out in a
tightening squeeze between the Department of Agriculture, which wanted to control the use of food in foreign
aid, and the Agency for International Development,
which wanted to control foreign aid policies regarding
food. Their lines to the White House were generally
clearer, certainly stronger. McGovern was a special assistant who had to clear his initiatives with other special
assistants.

It wasn't long before we felt like astronauts drifting
away from the mother ship, looking helplessly at the
fraying rope. That is the difference between "line" and
"staff." My father's definition of a well-run office is one in
which each person can concisely answer these questions:
Who reports to me? To whom do I report? What is my
job? Line can or should be able to answer them. Staff
never quite can. But staff has time for a few useful initiatives. Line has time for a generation of errors.

Not stillborn, then, but short-lived was the office of

Food for Peace. We did stimulate school-lunch and food-for-work programs, with grants of United States surplus food. Dealing at times directly with Governments, at other times through voluntary agencies like CARE, Catholic Relief, and Lutheran World Services, new and occasionally lasting attitudes were created abroad and at home about the utility and propriety of such aid. Yet within a year after George McGovern took on the assignment, our high hopes crested, leveled off, and began to recede. He ran for the Senate; I entered the Justice Department as administrative assistant to Attorney General Robert Kennedy. The Food for Peace office, under the able but circumscribed direction of Richard Reuter, the former head of CARE, was taken under the "protective" custody of the State Department. Agriculture and AID were free to prowl and spar again.

What is to be done to make the line agencies responsive to changes in the national perspective that new Presidents represent? Answer: the new Presidents—through their appointment of, and accessibility to, Cabinet officials willing to learn enough about their respective agencies to administer them. Whatever the value of intervening Presidential assistants to the formulation of sound policy, their privileged and detached status diminishes the morale of those charged with its implementation. Moreover, it is a jaded and costly Government that creates new line agencies rather than attempts to revive the old. The price for the seeming brilliance of such new creations is antagonism, jealousy, and destructive competition. Unable as history is to reveal its alternatives, we can only speculate whether Labor and HEW alone could have cooperated, or been made to cooperate in new ways, so as to carry on the brave new Poverty program. But if the often, too often, discredited OEO fails to pass its survival test, then its purely administrative cost was prohibitively high. The one limiting factor in the creation of new agencies is the size of the conference table in the Cabinet Room. There is no room for another chair.

What is accepted and what rejected is a mystery even in a democracy where not all truths are known, much less revealed—even to Congress. The 1969 hearings before the Space Committee of the House revealed dramatic changes in NASA programing dictated by nameless "experts" in the Budget Bureau.

The American people would like to be a great deal better informed than they are about what their Government does and why. They write thousands of letters a day to their representatives, requesting and cajoling. The amazing thing is they continue to do it in the belief that their exertions will be rewarded and their suggestions followed.

They could well be standing rank on rank on the Mall raising their voices in a majestic chorus of "where have all the ideas gone?" But they think they are getting through. They think so in spite of evidence to the contrary, clear evidence that even the highest officials have to struggle both to be heard and to be told. The Tonkin resolution should lay to rest the suggestion that the judgment of Congress, in vital matters, is always informed. In that particular case, even the President's judgment may not have been.

Congressional inquiry, then, should be considered a buffer and support for Executive curiosity, not a barrier or impediment. Even if one or both hear only what they wish to hear, their separate inquiries at least provide a useful balance. Applied to the same reports, then, their biases can compete on a fair field. I have mentioned the shell game that Congress, press, and public must play to uncover certain "foreign entanglements" such as the "Thai contingency plan," the rationale for our activities in Laos and Cambodia, and the military, including nuclear, bases we maintain across the world.

The people expect their elected representatives to know or to be able to quickly learn about the nation's foreign commitments. How else can intelligent debate ensue, opinion, ignorance, or error be exposed, or wise men be chosen? The Government is divided into locked compartments. There is really only one skeleton key—the President's. The press, however, has a good many that nearly fit, and in trying them one by one often force turnkeys to fling doors open and flee in a cloud of excuses. This power of the press is well understood by Government men who, finding themselves locked out, summon its aid in a variety of ways.

The keepers of the keys of public domestic responsibility can be equally secretive. In 1965–66 I served as executive director of the President's Committee on Juvenile Delinquency. My office was in the Justice Department. My rank was special assistant to the attorney general, who was designated chairman by the Executive order establishing the committee. The other two members were the secretaries of Labor and HEW. The committee's function was to coordinate the federal effort in combating delinquency. I discovered at the outset that in its four years it had never met. One afternoon I did bring it together, a great moment in bureaucracy.

The bewildered members, Attorney General Nicholas Katzenbach, Labor Secretary Willard Wirtz and HEW's John Gardner—three of the best men ever to serve in their respective posts—met, and with furtive staff aides tugging at their sleeves, conversed haltingly about their joint mandate.

"The great agencies of government," observed Secretary Wirtz, "don't like to be coordinated from the outside."

"Amen!" was the verdict accorded this unexceptionable pronouncement. The members parted in full agreement that the letter of the Executive order could not be fulfilled, but that the spirit of "sharing" information between the agencies should continue. That, at least, was a worthy objective.

Even that limited objective proved elusive. I learned, for example, that a profile of the racial and economic tensions of Watts, Los Angeles, had been prepared for HEW four years before the famous riot. I had the same success getting it sent to my office as Senator Fulbright had with the Thai contingency plan. I went to see it. It was lost that day. I persisted. I would have to ask Wilbur Cohen. Of course, I would talk to the phenomenal under secretary—the best informed man on welfare in America. All I wanted to see was the Watts study. Finally, I was allowed to "meet" a four-year-old study of tensions in Watts, coupled with recommendations that, if implemented, might have prevented that melee. More importantly, it would have provided an extremely valuable textbook on the anatomy of riots per se, together with ideas for their prognosis and treatment.

The American people can be proud of many government studies. We should simply insist that they not be buried alive. Why are they subjected to such indignity? In this case I think it was because, having been ignored beyond a relevant point in time (i.e., before the riot), it seemed only prudent not to call attention to a failure in initiative that could cost jobs.

Of course, the American people are more interested in good government work than safe government jobs. That is why Congress at least must find or fashion keys to these shy kingdoms, even if old friends crouch within, pleading for anonymity.

It is certainly easier to lose an idea in the bureaucratic maze than to find one. The euphoric Kennedy period was no exception. A veritable cornucopia of ignored initiatives, gathering for a decade, was there to open. But it had a small mouth, and keepers of the valves had to clear McGeorge Bundy for cold-war grand design and Europe, Michael Feldman for the Middle East and agriculture, Richard Goodwin for Latin America, Kenneth O'Donnell for special assistants who lacked their own key, Jerome Weisner for science, Theodore Sorenson for rhetoric, and Arthur J. Schlesinger for "new perspectives." Africa was left to the State Department until G. Mennen "Soapy" Williams suggested it be "for Africans," after which tighter controls were instituted. It was a tough line to rush, and no passing was permitted. Nevertheless, many a small fry tried his hand at drafting a play. As deputy director of Food for Peace, I prepared a paper for President Kennedy's use at his meeting with Premier Khrushchev in May, 1961.

I researched the Hoover Relief Commission's work in the Soviet Union, which followed Maxim Gorky's 1920 plea, made with the reluctant permission of the Bolshevik regime, for food from the West. Within a week of Gorky's request, American spokesmen landed at Riga and began negotiations which, in cooperation with the Russian government, were to result in shipments of food and medicine instrumental in saving the lives of some four million starving Russian citizens, including many children. There was good precedent, then, for U.S.–USSR peacetime cooperation.

In a memorandum to the President, with McGovern's approval and over his signature, I argued that this lesson in good will and cooperation between nations with different social systems, later allies in war, should not be lost at this threshold of a new day in Soviet–American relations. Laos, the then well-gnawed bone of contention between "elements" supported respectively by the United States and the Soviet Union, could serve as the basis for a new kind of cooperation. Neither side could consider conquest of the territory essential to survival. Otherwise, we would both be more overtly involved. The involvement of China would be unsatisfactory to either side. Why not, then, attempt to devise a cooperative effort to raise the standard of living in Laos and jointly influence the contending factions to effect at least a temporary reconciliation, leaving ultimate political questions to negotiations, plebiscites, or other arrangements besides warfare?

As the meeting would be held in Vienna, the capital of the one nation Stalin and the West jointly neutralized and freed, perhaps the spirit of Vienna could surface in other areas of the world where dangerous confrontation existed. Why should cooperation in "research," for example, be confined to cold climes like the Arctic? Why could not Russian doctors and technicians work with American colleagues in a jungle as well (a jungle later infested with North Vietnamese attracted by a vacuum of shared purpose)?

Actually Laos was a unique land, as ripe for exploitable divisions as for imaginative unifying efforts. It bordered six nations. From our point of view two were hostile, China and North Vietnam; two friendly, Thailand and South Vietnam; and two neutral, Burma and Cambodia. These numbered among the signatories of the later Laotian Accords of 1962, which did stress neutrality, but a neutrality susceptible of subversion by any interested kibitzers.

It is clear to us now that North Vietnam has proven the most interested, and has pursued that interest from the outset by failing to remove the 6000 troops she had there at the time, by adding some 50,000 to them since, by supporting Pathet Lao (Communist) attacks on the Government forces of Premier Souvanna Phouma who was chosen with the concurrence of Russia and North Vietnam, and by converting Laos' eastern sectors into an invasion route into South Vietnam. Only an active, not a passive, role in preserving Laotian neutrality could have served the great powers. Both the United States and the USSR preferred to stumble into a wider war than make the tough climb, roped together, toward a broader peace. Our joint paralysis has rendered subsequent efforts effective only to increase Hanoi's dependency on China.

The memorandum was dutifully fed and seen to disappear into the maw of the White House advisory team. Was it digested before it was eliminated? Certainly no such subject came up to warm the chilling encounter with Khrushchev, which left the most disarming man in American politics tight-lipped and pensive on his return. It also could have left the Soviet Premier with an underestimation of his adversary's resolve that may have influenced his Cuban moves a year later. The notes of American Ambassadors Llewellyn Thompson, Charles Bohlen, and George Kennan suggest that President

Kennedy was ill-prepared to debate Marxism with the Premier. By contrast it was the direct representatives of our "working class," Walter Reuther, George Meany, and others who left Khrushchev speechless in an encounter during his 1959 visit to the United States.

The cordon of experts with which an American President surrounds himself serves two purposes. One is to keep him necessarily informed. The other is to keep him necessarily uninformed. But the thousands of men and women who toil in the Executive Departments should be encouraged to think and suggest as well as sign off. And part of the necessary encouragement to innovation is the confidence that their department head, as a member of the President's Cabinet, has the ear and understanding of the President; that he does not read old *Time* magazines in the outer office of a White House helot, lately drafted to hold the pass against the President's own messengers. Many a reasoned memo has met its Thermopylae in this way.

And what began as a holding or screening action has taken on a more aggressive character. The tide of suggestion actually turns. Cabinet officers now return to their agencies not simply chastened, but "invigorated" with Presidential directives from the President's "man" on this or that. But the Cabinet member should be the President's man.

In addition to the Cabinet member, there are undoubtedly other competent men in his field who should be in Government. They should take his place or serve under him. This is only the more so as Government and the complexity of its problems grow. In a simpler time, perhaps, President James A. Garfield invited John Hay to serve as his personal assistant in the White House to help

him with difficult decisions. Hay declined. He said if he
were not up to the task of giving such advice he had no
business taking on such an assignment. On the other
hand, if he was that good a man, he would only come
between the President and his Cabinet, creating mistrust
and envy. "There are some decisions," wrote Hay in his
letter of declination, "a President must face alone."

Although that is still true today, the newly traditional
White House *cordon sanitaire* may operate to cause that
final decision to rest on misinformation, "bad transmission," and judgment restrained out of deference to false
prerogatives. The "White House team," a device to ease
the "loneliness of command," may, in effect, increase it.
A President should rather befriend his own first family,
his Cabinet, and take each member into his confidence.
For Cabinet members, the White House vestibule should
be an ante- not an anti-room. At that level of government,
mutual access should be natural and interdicted by an
absolute minimum of complications. The trouble is that
a lifetime of nonmeetings, for many of which they were
responsible, generally prepares even a Cabinet member
for disappointing relations with his colleagues and with
his President. The latter may derive relief from the
absence of problems short of urgent. Anticipating this,
his personal staff gladly absorbs the task of distinguishing
among problems. This being so, we should pray each
night not only for the President but for the men who
decide what or whom he shall see the next day.

Abraham Lincoln and some other early Presidents set
aside a time for citizens to pay calls. The country has
grown, but surely there is still Presidential time for Cabinet members. In the past two years we witnessed three
secretaries removed from their departments and part of

one department (Oceanography) removed from its secretary (Walter J. Hickel of Interior). Departmental employees and the public-at-large would be comforted to
believe that these removals did not stem from failure of
communication, or, more precisely, the absence of any
opportunity to communicate. Secretaries Robert Finch of
HEW and George Shultz of Labor accepted their respective changes in fortune with good grace. But while silence
may imply consent in law and White House shuffles, it
does not in the larger world of politics, self-appointed
spokesmen for the "silent majority" notwithstanding.
Silence may in fact harbor dissent or at best apathy. A
rightfully happy President is a listening one, and then
only when the people are encouraged to talk. Secretary
Hickel's encouragement came with his release. His famous
"letter," I feel certain, will be followed by a second shoe,
hobnail at that.

CHAPTER FIVE

It used to be said that talking to one's self was the first sign of insanity. True for an individual, perhaps, but not for a society. How to listen and how to speak to itself is a challenge for the North American community alone and for the whole society of American Republics, the Western Hemisphere. Each should listen to all its voices, not simply the loudest or nearest. Conscience itself speaks softly if, indeed, it is not trained, as Mark Twain once told Kipling, "to keep quiet."

Total immersion in Latin voices was offered by the conference to frame the charter for the Alliance for Progress, held at Punta del Este in August, 1961. Representatives from every Latin country were there, including a Cuban delegation headed by Che Guevara.

At the first general session, each delegation had a chance to offer preliminary remarks. Well-groomed ministers rose to the occasion, giving grand praise to the Kennedy initiative and the United States delegation, headed by Treasury Secretary Douglas Dillon.

Not so, Che. He rose in beret and fatigues, and began by laughing at the "so-called republic, the United States." Latin leaders, men whose position he threatened, were entranced. This is a familiar contradiction, when the United States is the butt of the joke. The United States, said Che, could think only of providing sanitation and bathrooms to the Latin peoples. For thirty minutes he dwelt on our preoccupation with plumbing. People wanted more than that, he went on. The audience, having in the first instance been led to accept his premise, followed him easily to his conclusion. He was a tremendous success. Dillon and the United States delegation sat glumly awaiting their turn. I was not a delegate, but an observer for the office of Food for Peace.

It seemed Che would wind up the winner of the opening event if our collars were too stiff, if we were solemn and bureaucratic, and dwelt solely on "programs." I wrote a note to Richard Goodwin suggesting we might remark in passing that it was not difficult to understand the apprehension of the Cuban representative concerning the installation of the named facilities. They would provide too tempting a receptacle for the daily decrees of his government. Mr. Dillon rose and stayed with the prepared text. He was politely received.

When the meeting broke up, Guevara was followed out into the street by spectators and ministers alike. In the aura of ancestral Latin resentment, which surrounds every conference with the Yankee colossus, he had achieved a substantive success that had cost him nothing.

That night, Che was the center of attention at the delegation dinner. Serious economists like the brilliant young Celso Furtado, who had fashioned a development plan for the destitute northeast of Brazil, pressed in to catch every word. It was Che's day. The young people stuck to him until his departure before the conference ended.

The next night we were all invited to a black-tie reception at the Museum. Fascinating paintings by Uruguayan

artists lined the walls of the beautiful old building.
Cocktails were served and commemorative medals
handed out by the proud mayor to all the delegates. I
noticed three less formally dressed young men in a corner. Long-haired and wearing open shirts, they looked
sullenly out on the crowd. I asked them what delegation
they were from.

"We are from the world of painters," said one of them.

"You mean you have done some of these works?" I
asked.

"Of course."

"But where are the others?" I asked.

"We were chosen to represent them at this." I told
them I would like to meet their friends and fellow-artists.
"You mean you would leave this place?"

"Yes."

In a few minutes we were stuffed into a 1929 Ford with
exposed engine, chuffing down a dirt road into the woods.
We pulled up at a pleasant looking house, and entered to
find fifty or so young men and women seated on the
living-room floor. They were being regaled by a bearded
fire-eater on *Yanqui imperialismo. Tenemos un Yanqui!*
shouted my escort. "We got one." The group fell silent.
Then one of them said, "Explain yourself." *No puedo sin
guitar*, "I cannot without guitar," I said. An instrument
was produced. I tuned it. I told a little about our folk
music, how it represented the growth and development
of the country, from wilderness to industry.

I sang and rambled for an hour or so, answered questions, had my grammar corrected. When it was late, they
stood and one by one shook my hand. It was then that I
finally met the hostess, Mrs. Elsie Rivero Haedo. She gave
her home over to "these spirits," she said, "to give them a

pleasant place to be forlorn and complain about life." It was better than the street. There was wine, comradeship, and "no foolish encounters" with police. "You," she said, "have made a change in them."

"Why?"

"Because you talked, you sang, you listened."

The next day one of the boys called me for more "talk." He had taken a painting to the Uruguayan President's palace and been rebuffed. He was sad. I went back and visited with them as the conference droned on. Then I walked the long beach.

August is winter in Punta del Este. The beach of reddish sand is deserted except for a few dead penguins. They reminded me of Western man in a dress suit washed up by the tide of history, and staring reproachfully heavenward, as if the blameless deity was responsible for his sad end. What could save the survivors, I wondered—more effort, more spirit. I sat down and wrote a few lines, found a guitar, and set them to music.

Alianza Para el Progreso	Alliance for Progress
Para cada hombre y nino,	For every man and child
Una gran hermandad marchando,	A great brotherhood marching,
Esperanza en cada corazon.	With hope in every heart.
Alianza para el progreso	Alliance for Progress
Quiere decir un esfuerzo	Means a force
Un esfuerzo grande y confiado	A force great and confident
Para ayudar al debil y olvidado.	To help the weak and forgotten.
Juntos conquistaremos;	Together we will conquer;
Los enemigos huirán muy pronto;	Our enemies will flee quickly;

Ignorancia, hambre, y miedo,	Ignorance, hunger, and fear,
Vencidos por los pueblos unidos.	Conquered by united peoples.
Aplaudimos, pues, el progreso.	Let's cheer progress then.
Formemos la gran alianza.	Let's form this great alliance.
Un alianza de esperanza,	An alliance of hope,
Ejemplo para el mundo,	An example for the world,
Alianza para el Progreso.	An Alliance for Progress.

That night, as the delegates gathered at the St. Raphael, I hooked one leg over the mezzanine balcony and sang the song.

The following March, on the anniversary of the Alliance announcement, President Kennedy held a reception in the East Room for all the Latin ambassadors and members of the Senate and House. Arthur Schlesinger called me. He said the President was worried the occasion would be a "bit stiff," and asked if I would sing "Alianza." When I arrived, the chief of protocol, Angie Duke, told me to relax; I would come on later. He was reversed, as I was so often to be in that post. The President, seeing me, asked me to come forward and start things off. He saw I needed a chair to put my foot on, and produced one, only just re-covered in yellow damask by Mrs. Kennedy. She was away, and I put my foot on it, lightly.

We all felt like singing in those days. We were full of hope and belief. We were not mindful of the last words of Simón Bolívar: "With my revolution, we have ploughed the sea." It closed in over ours as it did over his. We took arms against it, ploughed it, bailed it, and cused it. But it was as unresponsive as the Hellespont to the lash of Xerxes. What will history say about our

Yankee know-how? Nothing very kind in this regard until we prove we know *better* how. We need more Latin lessons.

For when Stokely Carmichael, sojourning in Havana, equated the "revolt" in the United States to the unrest in Latin America, he presented in characteristically blurred perspective a useful comparison. It is ironic that the voice of a strident expatriate should audibly resound in the North American community, which has demonstrated decades of deafness to the better voices to the south, voices which have had much to ask and to tell, but which, unheard or unheeded, have passed into silence with mild resignation—leaving the dialogue to the demagogue. Opportunities to listen to the better voices are not infrequent. In his essay, "The Pachuco and Other Extremes," the poet Octavio Paz wrote of the "Pauchucos," the young Mexican-Americans, he saw in Los Angeles.

The Pachuco does not want to become a Mexican again; at the same time he does not want to blend into the life of North America. . . . Since the Pachuco cannot adapt himself to a civilization which rejects him, he finds no answer to the hostility surrounding him except this angry affirmation of his personality. . . . The Pachuco actually flaunts his differences . . . he seeks and attracts persecution and scandal. It is the only way he can establish a more vital relationship with the society he is antagonizing.

As a victim he can occupy a place in the world that previously had ignored him; as a delinquent he can become one of its wicked heroes . . . I believe the North Americans' irritation results from his seeing the Pachuco as a mythological figure and, therefore, in effect, a danger.*

*This essay and later quotations of Paz (pp. 181, 246-47) appear in *The Labyrinth of Solitude*, translated by Lysander Kemp (Grove Press, Inc., New York, 1961), originally published in Mexico.

Some people, wrote Paz, credit the Pachuco with "unusual erotic prowess." He is a "symbol of love and joy, or of honor and loathing, an embodiment of liberty, of disorder, of the forbidden." Any contact with him must be made "in the darkness." He becomes in effect "a pariah."

The circle that began with provocation has completed itself, and he is now ready for redemption, for his entrance into the society that rejected him. He has been its sin and its scandal, but now that he is a victim it recognizes him at last for what he really is, its product, its son. At last he has found new parents.

This outline of the decline and rise of the Pachuco would need little editing to resemble a script of black America.

Paz wrote it before the emergence of "negritude," "black is beautiful," and the militant demands for separatism. In fact, he contrasted the Pachuco with the black he thought he knew, who "tries to enter the society." But with a poet's eye and pen, Paz has seen and told more in a few lines about the culturally alienated than many a social scientist in volumes of sententious com mentary.

Yet it is not so much by way of direct applicability to our own everyday problems that Latin voices speak. It is by a habit of thought, the perception of peripheral vision.

Granted few Latin nations have managed to forge one society within their borders—the legacy of a continental conquest by only two hundred thousand Spaniards. Yet Mexico has done so, and others are trying. Moreover, here in North America those who predict we are moving toward two societies are wrong. We have *been* a two-society nation, one white and vigorous and the other black and supine. If we are moving at all, we are moving away from a two-society to a one-society America. No one sees this with more clarity or opposes it with more vigor than the militants of the black community who lose more of their leadership position with every reconciling event. First the inarticulate, common sense of the black American will frustrate them. Then new and better leaders will replace them. This period of adjustment will not be uneventful, and those who demand tranquil acquiescence to legal pronouncements, devices, and injunctions cannot forget some bad examples that they may have countenanced in this regard.

Unresponsiveness to "lectures" as represented by court orders resulted, in fact, in the "Oxford Incident," the festive arrival of James Meredith on the campus of Mississippi University near the town of Oxford in September, 1962. We have heard a great deal from student militants, over the past year and more, demanding freedom from armed interference with their activities, amnesty for their transgressions, and a general hands-off policy during their demonstrations. They are rejected by many who demand instead the very kind of firm federal intervention they deplored in Oxford.

The Oxford incident was a student demonstration, aided and abetted by outside agitators, the arrival of many an informal vigilante group from Florida, Georgia, and Alabama, as well as the quaint, part-time leadership of Major-General Edwin A. Walker and the absentee encouragement of Governor Ross Barnett. It began with a court order supporting the personal suit of James Meredith to gain University admission as a Mississippian. The university was prepared to accept its first black student, but the Governor was not. After a series of complicated legal maneuvers the way was cleared for this historic matriculation, with only the details of time and place of arrival, in the company of federal marshals, to be worked out. As administrative assistant to Attorney General Kennedy, I heard him in a number of interesting telephone conversations with the Governor on this delicate subject. Most vivid was one of the last in which, in response to a suggestion of the Governor, Kennedy said, "You want one of the marshals to draw his gun, Governor? . . . That's dangerous, isn't it, Governor?" Yet he acquiesced and, when the conversation concluded, he explained to us the Governor did not feel that the state troopers and other Mississippi authorities could properly step aside until a symbolic act of threatened Federal force would justify it.

We were pondering the logic of that proposal when another call was put through. It was the Governor again. Kennedy picked up the receiver. ". . . all the marshals! You think all the marshals better draw their guns? . . . All right, Governor." He put the phone down, shaking his head. Arrangements were then made to effect a surprise arrival, earlier than expected, in order to avoid such a show-down with local lawmen.

It was in that same office Sunday evening, September 30, 1962, that we remained in telephone contact with the beleaguered Justice Department officials, headed by Deputy Attorney General Katzenbach, who had managed to escort Meredith onto the campus without incident by arriving ahead of the scheduled time. Having placed him under guard at a dormitory, without the knowledge of the campus community, they made their headquarters at the Faculty Lyceum which conveyed the impression

that Meredith was still in their custody. History records
how student "militants" gathered and, joined and urged
on by buffoons from a surrounding four-state area, began
tossing rocks at the marshals guarding the Lyceum premises. We recall how the numbers grew to nearly two
thousand, the curses, threats, some firing, and finally the
Molotov cocktails in bottles normally containing the
"pause that refreshes." The ring closed around the some
185 marshals, many of whom had been struck by flying
glass, some seriously wounded. At about 8 P.M., just as the
President was making his radio appeal for peace and
order, the marshals fired their tear gas. Some canisters
fell at the feet of the local and campus police. This
removed any vestige of remaining interest on their part
to quiet or discipline the crowd. I listened to the President with one ear, and with the other to my colleague,
Harold Reis, who was reclining beneath a desk in the
Lyceum reporting the conflict. The marshals, to their
credit, never drew their sidearms, although they must
have been tempted. One was dying from loss of blood.
The ambulance sent for was stopped at the gate, and
only permitted to proceed if the driver would pledge he
wasn't going for one of those "damned" marshals. A fire
truck was commandeered by some of the more adven-
turous "student demonstrators" and driven toward the
marshals, being boarded and barely turned away seconds
before it would have crushed some of them. Troops
arrived and made their way through the streets of Oxford
through a gantlet of hurled brick and broken curbstone.
Late that night I was ordered to fly there, help with the
questioning of armed suspects, and try to establish some
better communication with local authorities.

Landing by helicopter in the army encampment amidst

trucks, jeeps, and troops, I was driven by a marshal who advised holding my coat over my head to avoid the results of a broken window. The campus was a battle-field scene—tear gas still heavy in the air; young soldiers nervously patrolling, picking their way through over-turned cars; empty tear-gas canisters; broken glass and torn clothing. Marshals slumped in sleep; clusters of young men sat under guard. I interviewed a good many of them. I asked them why they thought this business had happened; surely one black student wouldn't destroy the university.

One big fellow said, "My daddy told me." Another replied, "My preacher could explain you." Still another said his parents had called during the riot. He had assured them he was safe in his room and not involved. "What?" roared his father. "You get out there and fight for your university like a man!"

I called on the ministers of the Oxford area. They differed in attitude and resolve. One young preacher from Georgia said there were two kinds of laws in the area, those which were observed and those which were not. Laws protecting Negroes were one of the latter. The students, he said, generally would have no rationale for their race views, but would indeed defer to home teach-ing or their preacher. There was no campus ethic as distinct from homegrown biases refreshed on weekend visits home. I asked if there wasn't some approach to reason. He replied, "Not with emotions you don't rea-son." One must substitute other emotions, and must be a Mississippian besides. He, a Georgian, felt like an alien at times. Another minister passed on to me a telephone lineman's report that "hillbillies" were camping in the woods waiting for the troops to leave so they could come in for Meredith. A third preacher met me smiling, bright-eyed. He had preached an anti-Federal sermon the pre-ceding Sunday, which had been published in the Oxford paper. He discoursed on the historical and Biblical justification for opposing "tyranny." I asked what kind of government the state must appear to be to nonwhites. He replied it was better to have "a lot of little tyrannies—indigenous to the locale—than one big one."

"Restoring" communication with local authorities would have been difficult had it not been for their own initiative. On Thursday, October 4, Ken Faulkner, the university bursar, worked his way past the marshals at the door of the Faculty House to convey an invitation to "any Federal representative" to speak at the Lions Club luncheon in town that day. I accepted. Nick Katzenbach concurred. There was some discussion of television cover-age, but I felt this was not the time for it. Faulkner, a tall, soft-spoken man, and I walked through the campus to his car. Soldiers were patrolling in full battle dress; jeeps moved slowly through the area. Helicopters roared overhead. Students on their way to classes joshed the young, self-conscious troops. Dozens of newspapermen milled around the headquarters. We had moved all the better furniture upstairs.

Arriving at the Mansion Restaurant, Faulkner escorted me past the ticket lady.

There were about fifty businessmen, tradesmen, some in their 20's and 30's, others much older. I went around the tables and shook hands. They were cordial, a typical service-club group. The mayor, Richard Elliot, was there, and some ministers. There were a few reporters, includ-ing James Rogers of the *Herald Tribune* who told me later they couldn't believe I would do it.

I was introduced as an assistant to the attorney general
—and the audience was told that the chairman hadn't
discussed the subject of my talk with me. I told them I
hadn't discussed it with myself, and that I was aware that
I could become a "wholly disowned subsidiary" of the
Justice Department. I mentioned that hungry as I had
been over the past few days (cold C rations out of a can),
their chairman may have wondered why I hadn't eaten
more lunch. But I presumed they could guess why!

I said, "You may be wondering why we're here," and
explained that we were there not because we had filed a
suit, but because a suit had been filed—to which we were
not even a party—and that the courts, all of them, had
spoken and said all they could say, and that the reaction of
certain key persons involved made it necessary for the executive branch of government to play a rather more active
part than usual in securing conformance with the court's
order.

Being from Missouri—a state where all orders of all
courts were not only accepted, but unanimously acclaimed
by people parading in an orderly fashion in the streets—a
state where there has never been one recorded violation of
law—I naturally appeared before them with a clear
conscience.

So, I said, we came on orders—and what did we find
when we came? We found a fine town, a great university
with some confused students and faculty, and what else?
Strangers—like us but not like us, for we had come to work
out peaceful solutions and the other strangers had not
come for this.

These were men who had no family here, no future
here, no business here—except the miserable business of
leading young men with both family and future into the

kind of behavior that could ruin their future and sadden their families. Having joined in some student rallies myself, I remembered the attraction, but it was an activity not to be encouraged by adults whether in public or in private life. Yet even in students, I said, there was usually a residual sense of responsibility. It hadn't been called upon. It hadn't been used.

I said it seemed to me that this group of men were men whose values and hopes could set a proper standard for the youth of this area. And we needed their help. No law, no court, no government could provide the exact kind of leadership that was needed. It rested with them and in them. And I felt that this town, this university, would be exactly what its people, its students, wanted it to be, both proud and law-abiding, which itself is a source of pride.

In closing, I said that one of the problems of residents of small cities is in finding an answer to the frequent question, "What's new?" I said I thought they would agree they had solved that problem for the moment, and would probably appreciate having it back again. I said that I was very grateful for the invitation they, through their chairman, had conveyed, and that I hoped they would feel free to call on us to advise us and to let us know how we could do our job better and make theirs easier. Then some questions followed:

"When will the troops leave?" I said this again depended on them (the townspeople, etc.). It was a question I would have to refer back to them.

"If I don't obey, do I go to jail?" one fellow asked. I had no problem here since all the others yelled joyfully, "Take him—good riddance."

"Why the colored troops?" I said the Army is not a political body and arranges its units without such consider-

ations. (Actually, the black troop levels were cut back—
very much so. One fellow had noticed and said, "There
don't seem to be so many now." I said, "Really?")

"Why stop cars?" I said we needed to isolate, if possible,
and prevent falling into wrong hands weapons and ammu-
nition. I said I realized most of these weapons were carried
for normal purposes, and this was the "huntingest town I
ever saw," but I added that it would be more convenient if
these guns could be left at "the lodge." Also, it was not
clear to me how many squirrels were likely to be dispatched by machetes, samurai swords, and baseball bats
with nails driven through them. I also reported suggesting
that the troops inspecting cars check the oil and gas, but
was informed that was not in their instructions.

The men were generous. The Mayor rose and thanked
me on behalf of the club. He added that while they hadn't
welcomed the arrival of James Meredith they were even
less hospitable to the violence that occurred. He felt that
the presence of troops was salutary for the time being.

One of the younger men invited me for dinner. I
accepted, and walked again that evening through the campus, still with the unpleasant sensation of being a not-so-
honored prophet in another land. I was met in the
doorway of the small, frame home. In the background
were a dozen or more young men and women. My host
handed me a large tumbler of bourbon, filled to the top.

"How about some ice?" I asked.

"We don't water our drinks here," he said.

The meal was to be squirrel, and particular interest was
taken in showing me the culinary details of its preparation. The entire squirrel, skinned, is rolled in aluminum

foil and placed in the oven for an hour or so. The hour was spent downing the contents of the tumbler and undoubtedly others. The conversation became animated. A guitar was produced and I sang some songs for them. When the squirrels were ready, I was closely watched for my reactions. The pièce de résistance is the brain, a generous glop of white, marrow-like matter, recessed in the head, naturally, and secured by probing with a small fork. I realized this was an important test and the sooner met the better. I went for it immediately, speared it, and plopped it deep in my throat in order to bypass as much as possible my apprehensive taste buds. It was a success; the "damn Yankee" was "all right." If that was true, I derived a good deal of the necessary stamina from the aforesaid tumbler.

I do believe, in looking back over other scenes, that temperance is highly useful. But temperance is not a guarantee of tolerance. I have known people who will not smoke, drink, or curse, but tolerant they are not. Conversely, the kind of conversation that draws deeply on what the participants feel, even if their feelings differ, is not ill served by a little reasonable lubrication.

At the evening's end, or the morning's beginning, which was more the case, we exchanged heartfelt good byes; we all agreed to "think about" what we had said. I walked erect back to the Faculty Club, and had a short nap before sunrise. As I think back, I liked those people.

It's hard to know what you've left behind in the way of a memory or impression. But months later in Washington, Senator John Stennis stopped me in a Capitol corridor, said he'd "heard about" what I'd done, and wanted to thank me. I told him the people were good to me, and they were.

One of the oddities of the week of the disorders was the appearance of Hal Holbrook as Mark Twain in the university auditorium. Before a packed house of students, he went through the famous monologues that twitted racism. The audience was completely responsive, saw the points, and laughed every minute. Could these be the same youngsters who continued to jeer Meredith on the tree-lined walkways between classes? Meredith was certainly not considered out of danger, and was under guard for a month or so. During the second week, I flew "escort" with him in a light plane to Jackson so he could visit his family. He was detached, undemonstrative, and not particularly impressed with the herculean Federal effort to keep him alive and in school. We drove to his house, and the marshal promised to bring the car back in three hours for the return trip. I had supposed that I would go in with him. I should have realized that I would not be invited; I sat out on the sidewalk for that period.

Later, I visited lawyers, publishers, and businessmen throughout the state of Mississippi. It was clear that whatever satisfaction we may have taken in having enforced a court order, it was an expensive and awkward way to do it. The Governor had apparently reached a low ebb of popularity before the event, and had now been catapulted right up to the top again. Mississippians who opposed his handling of the affair urged that he not be further martyred. In retrospect, I cannot but believe there was another way. Briefly, Kennedy and Barnett should have met, taken refreshment together, and exhausted their personal resources before committing their institutional resources. In the aftermath of the events scheduled by the relentless logic of noncommunication, neither side could have taken satisfaction. Yet it was not an unpredictable "happening," given the ingredients present—a volatile atmosphere, deep-seated resentments, and a massive movement of

Federal force. If elements such as these can stifle reason and restraint here in this country, how can we expect to achieve peaceful resolution of conflicts abroad?

It may have come down to the character and ambitions of a governor. But he was human, too, not unsusceptible, I should think, to the suggestions of a deputation of the very leading citizens with whom I spoke following that tragic week. We cannot accomplish this kind of meeting, barking orders in a phone, and swirling in desk chairs in the paneled offices of Washington.

Had the Governor been unmoved by diplomatic representation of any kind, he might have been reminded of a previous (1850) Mississippi governor, John Quitman, a Mexican war hero who, having aided military missions to Cuba to assist the revolutionary Lopez wrest the island from Spain, was indicted for violation of neutrality laws. He appeared on his balcony to state to his people that he knew not whereof he had offended any law, but would not oppose the modest power of his people against irresistible Federal force and suffer the futile bloodshed that would ensue. On the other hand, he could not subject the sovereignty of his state in his person to the indignity of submission to legal process, so out of respect for his people, he would relinquish the high responsibility they had reposed in him. Resigning, he was taken to New Orleans for trial, acquitted, returned, and was elected to Congress, higher than ever in the respect of his people. It is not known whether his latter-day successor considered this alternative, but it might not have been a bad example to follow.

Citizens rampant on a field of national indecision make an unsightly coat of arms for a country. And we should not underestimate the likelihood of further confrontations when school desegregation, food stamp, and welfare regulations pinch some nerves. Nor should we judge Mississippi harshly. There, but for certain circumstances, challenges, and leadership, goes any state, north and south. What the Federal departments need are patient, sensitive men, with the vision to perceive what the law requires and the tact and deference to make others think they saw it first. Still, governing through reason cannot be achieved until the people governed have come to accept a common denominator of public responsibility in relation to private expectation. This they cannot do until they have come to understand it is in their long-term best interest. No such understanding is possible until they have met one another, broken bread together, laughed, and shared the cementing experience of mild self-ridicule. Until then, it is all thrust and parry and forget it.

CHAPTER SIX

Who are the folks who, silently or not, elect Presidents and expect great things of them? They are we, certainly, but who "we" are is something "we" don't know. For example, we are no longer merely descendants of persecuted and persevering English pilgrims. We have, in fact, gone through a number of persecutions since then. But we each savor our own deliverance, and are not comfortable with any other.

A constituent strongly favoring the ABM wrote me during that debate, "We must forget about our social turmoil, the Negro question, and such issues, and think about survival." It seemed more like an epitaph than a suggestion. I wondered in reply what nation in history ever "forgot" about its social turmoil and survived. We seem to wish to live in compartments behind our "good fences." Progress is measured by the development of better fences. The olo New Englander would certainly be impressed to look up from his crude workmanship and see an ABM emplacement. There's a good fence for you, impervious, if it works, to a certain level of skyborne gate crashers, if not to the suitcase bomb. But as we bend to the task of erecting this new generation of weapons we should think of the next generation of children who will be made "secure"

by them, and ask ourselves if that security won't depend
more on openings than closures of the human spirit,
human society, and the world community. The day of the
siege society and its castle keep is gone.

Yet few of us know how the gate works in minds other
than our own, or in those of similar bias. Since the accumu-
lation of views within those gates constitutes the collective
concern of the electorate, there is one breed that must try
them all—the campaigner. No one is in a better position to
report on the talk in America than the political campaigner. Only barbers and cab drivers share equivalent
confidences. Journalists, since they can be, generally are
more selective. Thus, whether the campaign ends in
victory or defeat, it is a unique education for the contenders. Unfortunately only a few people seek public office,
and some, among the few, hide what they see and stifle
what they hear. If we could report more effectively and
honestly, we might compete with the literary world in
previewing the surprises society has in store for itself. A
public man should serve as a convener of people who have
never met. It is certainly difficult to establish a consensus
of public opinion if the people who constitute the public
won't talk with each other.

In the months leading to the elections of November,
1968, I spent hours listening to reactions to stronger gun
laws. "Guns don't kill; people do," and "when guns are
outlawed, only outlaws will have guns," were prevalent
slogans in the white community. At the same time black
leaders familiar with such white attitudes, had come somewhat resignedly to fear, if not anticipate, the same ultimate confrontation—don't fire till you see the eyes of the
whites—and did not want to face it unarmed. Moreover,
unlike the white community, the black community

doubted registration laws would be administered fairly on its behalf. Projecting other experiences with city hall authority, the blacks foresaw the minor discrepancies that would be discovered in their applications, the juvenile record, the unpleasant run-in with a traffic officer, the inability to produce certificates of birth, testimonials, character references, or whatever the local market required. No, indeed, they would not trade the relative freedom they now had to purchase weapons for the false promise of security offered by registration requirements.

Some in the white community, being apprised of black feeling in this matter, were tempted to reconsider. They were clearly bemused by the prospect of registration laws which, contrary to their bumper slogans, would actually strengthen their relative position in the domestic arms race. The question is relevant to the international arms race. If we don't trust one another well enough at least to register our little guns, why should others have confidence in our big gun policy?

What does all this suggest to the sane American, black or white? To me it points up the importance of exposing in both communities the barren point of view of each, bringing home to each the folly of such escalation of suspicion and hate in the one land in the world where the ability of races to live together in peace is being tested with every advantage—rule of law, unequalled economic growth, a history of common sense, and a destiny that has enthralled mankind. The first childish thing to put away is unreasonable fear. Knowledge can dispel such fear— knowledge of each other. Nor should we accept quick assumptions as knowledge even, and perhaps in particular, when these assumptions are offered by self-appointed spokesmen. "Please don't understand me too quickly," a philosopher wrote. It will take a while for all of us to learn. Meanwhile, what blacks want, or what whites want, must not be left to a few of each to decide and declaim. The education of the American black, given its obstacles, has taken a long time. The education of the American white, given its obstacles, will not take a short time. The work stoppages in Pittsburgh and demands for equality in construction hiring practices occurred more than a year after a conversation I had with a young "dissident" of St. Louis County.

"Jobs, man," is what he said. He was the tallest of the thirty or more young men in their late teens and early twenties languidly leaning on parked cars on the main street of Kinloch, a black community in St. Louis County. You know when you've entered Kinloch because the paving stops and the ruts slow you down.

Pride in this town of 10,000 was taken in the fact that sewers had finally been installed, albeit improperly so streets were buckling. Other problems remained, and I wanted to know how they rated them. As I walked up to the group, they drew together and looked at me curiously. I greeted them, told them I was a first-time candidate for Congress, and that I was just visiting.

"What you going to do for us?" asked the big one, pleasantly.

"I'm not sure what I can do; I wonder what you can do," I replied. "What is the biggest need here?"

"Jobs, man," he said.

I asked him what kind of jobs they thought they could handle.

"Construction. Whitey comes, puts in public housing, sits on the roof and bangs on the shingles. We can do that, but he just takes his payroll and goes home with it. We

just watch. And what's left? The public housing doesn't
pay taxes, so anybody living in their own houses got to pay
more taxes."

"What else?" I asked.

"Recreation—a place to go, like the schoolyard in evenings. We can't go in there because we vandalize, they say.
And there's no center or anything around here, so we stay
out here on this corner until the cop comes and tells us to
move. Then we move over there on that corner. When he
gets there, we move back."

I had been told that the crime rate, particularly bur-
glary, was high in the area, and that many families were
afraid. Yet it was as popular in some sections of the county
to suggest that poverty and crime were related as it was to
tell the tobacco industry years ago that smoking was hazardous to health.

"What local officials do you admire?" I asked.

The boys were standing loose now, relaxed. "Admire?"
said the big one. He laughed heartily with the others. "No
one, man."

I named the few I knew, and they just shook their heads.
"Well, is there anyone in a position of authority here that
you trust?" I asked.

"No, not one," he said.

Just then we heard a horn, a screech of brakes, and a
thump. We turned in time to see a battered old Buick pick
up a little boy, and send him head over heels twenty feet
to where we stood. We ran to him. He lay twisted, his
bleeding cheek on the gravel; his eyes were all fear and
pain. We pillowed his head, and I put my coat over him.
One of the boys went into the hamburger stand to call.
People gathered quietly. Our gaily painted campaign bus
and the straw-hatted youngsters stood to one side. Police

came, two black officers. They questioned the driver. The
mother came and cried, and bent over the boy, but no
doctor, no ambulance. After thirty minutes we prevailed
on the officers to take the boy and his mother in the squad
car to the hospital. We lifted him gently into the back seat;
he was whimpering. His mother held him. They drove off.

"If that'd been me," said the big fellow, "I'd be lying
there yet."

"What do you mean?" I asked.

"Like I say, the police never take the hurt people, unless
they're small like him, or somebody like you standing
around." The boys drifted away with the rest of the crowd.
They didn't seem to have much confidence in their
"America."

A week or so later I was working at the campaign headquarters when a determined little lady strode past the ban-
ners and placards for a "word with the candidate." "I'm
seventy-five years old, and I want to know what's going
on in this country," she said. "All this welfare, and you
can't get an able-bodied man or boy to mow your lawn or
take the trash." She went on. "I know things are difficult,
but they were for me, too." In old world accents she
described how she had come to this country from Romania
in 1906 with her widowed mother, how they clutched the
ship's rail as the Statue of Liberty loomed hugely in the
mist, the sixth floor walk-up, cold-water flat, and the
mother's job in a bank scrubbing floors until she died on
her knees with the brush in her hand. By then her daughter had learned to sew, and worked in a dress shop, which
she later supervised before coming to St. Louis. "It was
hard," she said, "but we managed. What's the matter with
people nowadays?"

As she left I thought about the "man or boy" who

couldn't be found to mow a lawn or take the trash, but who, miles away, wanted to build houses. What vivid recollections of hope, trial, and adventure did they have? What ancestral memories? Who were their forefathers, and what brave ship brought them into what harbor? What lamp was lifted beside what golden door? For them, no salt spray on the fresh winds of freedom, but sweat, foul odors, darkness, and chains. Perhaps easier forgotten, but a memory that should be reached for by all of "us."

It was during this period that my mother gave me a book to read, *Ishi—Between Two Worlds* by Theodora Kroeber. It is the story of a California Indian, the last of a scattered tribe with a prehistoric culture. In 1911, after the ranchers and posses had hunted and killed every member of his family, he threw himself on a fence and the mercy of the marauding conquerors. Emaciated and speaking no known tongue, he was first taken to jail for display and study as the "wild man." Luckily, an anthropologist, Alfred Kroeber, working at Berkeley, heard of him, came, and took him into his care.

The book, written with gentle strength by Kroeber's widow, recounts in detail the way in which communication began between Ishi and his twentieth-century friends. Ishi, about forty years old, had a Stone Age understanding of the world about him, but a sound judgment about people. With a sensitivity to human nature he chose his companions carefully. Kroeber he admired, and strove to please. A few others got to know him well, but the indecent laughter and low-caste humor of some of the "house" Indians and half-breeds of the community were distasteful to him. He recognized and sought men with dignity. Ishi lived only briefly in willing captivity, before civilization conferred its final gift on him, fatal tuberculosis.

Perhaps because the pain of parting was too much to articulate, there were no words "good bye" in Ishi's language, only "I go, you stay." He left his sorrowing friends calmly, giving them and all of us new perspective on the primitive and the "civilized."

Early in his relationship with Kroeber and his fellow scientists, Ishi, having been shown where he could buy candy at the store, accepted an "allowance" of small change for such purchases. One day, inexplicably, he refused the money, and did not go. Late that night he was discovered sweeping the floors of the building as he had seen the janitor do. The next day he smilingly took his money. Human pride is primeval.

But the most revealing thing about Ishi was his name itself; what it told, and what it hid. Ishi was the tribal word for "man!" A personal name was too sacred to share with strangers, good as they might be to him. Ishi's precious name was for his family only to know. If asked who he was, a member of Ishi's tribe would answer, "I am a person." This was enough to know as the basis for further communication. To tear from a man his name would be insulting, degrading. I think of the Romanian immigrant and her linear struggle for a stable life in America, the long chain of remembered pride and effort, link by link, stretching back beyond memory, forward beyond dreams. Here is a person, certainly, confident of her identity and never threatened with the loss of it.

What about the boys in Kinloch? When seen in the light of his total experience in this "new world," it is no wonder that the black American seeks to regain his identity. The wonder is he could have delayed so long, and the greater wonder it is that a society so normally alert to the needs of groups and individuals did not recognize this need, and do something about it sooner. Perhaps the delay has been due to the former passivity of the demand, and the diverting challenges of war and national growth. Or it might be due in some extent to the twin assumptions of white America: one, that any man can make it in this democratic new world; two, that some are destined to be left a little behind. Understandable, then, is the clamor for black studies in the schools and colleges, lectures and seminars on black art and culture. So is the emergence of Afro styles, the search for an authenticity, not patterned to emulate or divert the descendants of "ole massa," but to remind us all that every man is descended from the noble as well as the tawdry, and justified to choose; that every man can be determined to *ascend* to a prouder future.

Far from bucking the trend, we should advance it, prepare a place for it in our minds, and welcome it. Certainly a nation half-proud, and half-ashamed, cannot endure. It is better, more satisfying, and safer to live among a proud people than a humiliated people. How this new-found pride will come to fit in the American pattern of motivation, happiness, and "success," time will tell. The first thing to avoid is the idea of giving "dignity" to others. Dignity is not for anyone to give, but is in everyone to recognize. Nor should troubled people be too quickly "understood" and naive encouragements offered their worst leadership. The strident militants exploiting the nameless fears of the black poor with misplaced white "liberal" support would, if they could, produce a new generation of Uncle Tom-Toms who would beat out rhythms and step and fetch for a black demagogue as readily as their ancestors did for the house on the hill. The similarity is too plain to go unnoticed. But self-awareness is personal as well as collective.

In the spring of 1969, during a downtown St. Louis celebration, a young man introduced himself to me. Then, as steel guitar music ricocheted around us, he said, "Look at me; am I black?" I studied his face. "Come on— am I black?" he insisted.

I told him he really looked brown to be precise.

"Right," he exclaimed. "The only thing black about me is my hair."

"Your hair is black," I agreed.

"Lots of people have black hair," he pointed out.

"They do," I said.

"Good talking to you," he said.

"Same here, any time," I replied. And we went back to our respective tables. Later, I joined him and we talked about other things.

The first decently educated generation of black America will disdain cakewalking to any fool's tune. In the meantime the level of receptivity to the range of suggestions of latter-day Nat Turners will depend on the total context for living that America provides. We should be careful also not to confuse true roots with the roots of cultural patronization. In some new school programs, English is dealt with as a mere alternative to "real talk," the unstructured street expression of the black poor. "Real talk" is encouraged for the sake of confidence. Such confidence will be short-lived. These people come to the city for jobs and better schooling, not to trade their rural dialect, which provided amusement to generations, for an urban one. There is no premium today on quaintness. If Pat Moynihan's statement to the President that only 16 per cent of black high school graduates have even a grade school level command of verbal skills is anywhere near correct, the proponents of the two-society nation must be well pleased. Computers and personnel offices are programed in English, not "real talk." The schools must realize this.

What about the schools? At a late summer picnic in Kinloch some parents told me they dreaded the coming of fall, and the new crop of young, low-paid teachers who would last a year or two before quitting for a better post. The turnover gave no chance for continuity and the steady growth of respect that builds like coral around the teacher who taught a big brother, a cousin, perhaps a father. No school can be built on such quicksand; more importantly, no student. Sometimes where teachers have stayed on, it is due not to faith and commitment, but inertia. Such teachers come to expect and demand progressively less from each successive class.

My wife taught music as a volunteer in a Washington public school. It was an experiment to see if the fourth grade children could benefit from it. There were three sections or "tracks" of thirty each, and rated slow, medium, and fast, based on tests and the regular teacher's perception of each child's general knowledge and aptitude. My wife was told at the outset not to "expect much from these kids." I saw her each day leaving the house with an armload of books, papers, a wooden keyboard, and an autoharp. There was no piano at the school.

She loved it. There was talent in each "track." She got them singing rounds and parts. I joined them one day. They were an "up" group. At Thanksgiving time my wife suggested they learn the Thanksgiving hymn by heart. This was too much for the regular teacher. "They can't," she said. "It's too hard for them; they will be disappointed in themselves. After all, how could they understand 'chas-

tens and hastens His will to make known'?" She was not
moved by the reminder that most children sing the song
many times without understanding every word. Yet the
youngsters learned it quickly and sang it lustily. "The
education of heroes," wrote Plato, "begins with music."

At that same time in 1966 I wrote an article for *The
Reporter* magazine on "Youth, Crime and the Great
Society." In it I discussed some facets of our approach to
errant youth, the institutions we commit them to, and the
example we set them. As it has relevance, I think, to youth,
not necessarily errant, but growing and wondering, I
quote from it here:

We are a young country and getting younger. Within a few
years half of all American citizens will be under twenty-five.
The median age is already down to fifteen in Latin America.
There, teen-agers in urban and rural ghettos carry their smaller
brothers or sisters on their back for miles to the doctor or for
safe drinking water. The challenge of living to help others and
the effort it requires keep many such youngsters on a straight
if rocky road. Our own children, rich and poor alike, want to
feel involved in causes that transcend themselves, their community, and their time. For many, the chance to help develop
and carry out neighborhood programs of education or recreation would provide such a cause. . . .

And what happens to those adolescents whom "programs,"
however well conceived and executed, fail to sway? What of
the "institutions" that receive them and the courts that send
them there? James Bennett, former director of the Federal
Bureau of Prisons, recalls that less than five per cent of the
Federal judges in his time ever visited a Federal prison. How
many juvenile court judges have made a thorough investiga-
tion of the institutions to which they entrust their charges?
But why stop with judges? How many mayors, aldermen,
councilmen, or state legislators have really investigated the

institutions to which juveniles are committed? And if they are found wanting, what higher priority could there be for the expenditure of public funds?

It is not a question of comforts. One director proudly claimed that "his boys" could watch television every night and see two movies a week. Undoubtedly they were doing that at home when they should have been working, studying, or listening to music that was written from the head and heart and not the mid-section. We must ask what demands are being made of these kids, demands that will stretch their minds and lift their spirits, rather than pap to dull them into sullen acceptance of their lot. . . .

Last December 23, [1965], with Solicitor General Thurgood Marshall and Federal Bureau of Prisons Director Myrl Alexander, I stood in the dining hall of the National Training School for Boys. We were being shown the school's kitchen and dining facilities. The boys—about two hundred of them—ate quietly, some glancing in our direction. One motioned us over.

"We just wanted to wish you a Merry Christmas," he said, "and to ask who the hell you were."

We wonder who the teen-ager in trouble is. He wonders who we are and what hypocrisies we conceal, what crimes we permit to be perpetrated on his family that undermine its faith in society and law: the quiet crimes of con men who victimize the poor, the new breed of Medicare parasites, the contractor who says he represents Urban Development and must improve the home to save it from condemnation, the bank that takes the note on such transactions. . . . This is what makes a job a tough one for the policeman, who is seen by the poor more often as the enforcer of laws that take rather than protect. . . .

The headlines on delinquency itself bring many a fist down on many a breakfast table. They stimulate letters to Congressmen and other acts of futile indignation. In fairness, second section reports of slum conditions and recommended community action also stimulate our big-hearted apathy—not only with respect to those elements of society which prey on the less fortunate but also with respect to our own homes and the examples and standards we set for our own children. We talk about excellence and the pursuit of excellence. But how many adult Americans are growing breathless in the pursuit of excellence? Consider the shameful dross that the average adult community accepts as commonplace and be grateful, if incredulous, that the proportion of the young who lose sight of our highest standards to the extent of violating our lowest is under five per cent. Aristotle counseled that children should not be permitted to be "spectators of vice or hate."

We permit our children to be spectators of vice and hate every day. To forbid it would be attacked as deprivation of some Constitutional right on the part of the purveyors of vice and hate. Worse than that, it would require self-discipline on our part. But in permitting it, we do give our children some hard choices, and ourselves too. For we have the choice of whether or not to ignore the consequences of the double standard we so calmly observe. As long as this is the case, the teenager of our time is tempted to inquire what is "like so great" about our society.

Few of us actively seek to expose our cherished presumptions to the hazards of inquiry—particularly when they relate to the young, the poor, or the black. When we are ready to do so, we too often turn to mere "dialogue." Many a one-way trip has been taken from "dialogue" to disappointment.

The impenetrable barriers of our time will succumb, we are told, to dialogue. It reminds me of the slogan for a former hair "restorer," Herpicide. "Going? Herpicide will save it! Going? Herpicide will save it! Gone? Too late for Herpicide." Substitute "Dialogue" for "Herpicide," and you have the current rationale, if not panacea, for saving "it"—peace, racial harmony, or what you will. I doubt it.

Dialogue as often practiced can be a barrier to understanding. The dialogues of the sixties, like those of the centuries, have tended to preserve, not end, suspicion and hostility. Like Herpicide, dialogue has lacked the ingredients to do the job. What are the ingredients of effective dialogue? It is said that "the body travels more easily than the mind, and we haven't taken one step until we have taken up residence in another person's point of view." Dialogue isn't a tennis match with truth as the ball, to be "put away" with a telling stroke. That's debate; the results are favorable to the pro no matter how earnestly and deservedly the amateur places his shots.

Dialogue to be useful must be an event that none wins unless all win; that can merge and synthesize the ideas of the amateurs and the pros, Ph.D.'s, and illiterates, the angry, the timid, the prayerful, and the iconoclast; and that can make them all believers in the process, if not each result. There should be no "sides" chosen at the outset.

Most thoughtful whites express racial views that would not unite any white community. Nor are the publicized differences of Carmichael and Cleaver more than one tip of one iceberg of black controversy. The black Africans of the dark continent have manifest problems "meeting" their cousins over here. I presented a black American official to an African diplomat in my home. They approached one another stiffly, backs arched, arms outstretched with diffident acknowledgment. Both were cultivated men, but after circling warily over a few pleasantries they each withdrew to the comfortably familiar biases of the white America they each "knew" in their own way.

American blacks speak their distrust of the pan-Africa pretensions of some African leaders who put more faith in guns than fertilizer, jails than parliaments, peonage than tractors. On the other hand, I have heard African diplomats deride the American black for failing to cast off the last of his chains. One thinks of the other as a bush despot, and in turn is dismissed as a latter-day slave. No, for dialogue to be useful here we will need a little more *self-deprecation* than the kind that is offered. To bring together men who have never met, who control power, and who have no current basis for mutual trust is a difficult undertaking. "Does it not seem," wrote Emerson in his essays on manners, "as if man was of a very shy, elusive nature, and dreaded nothing so much as a full rencontre front to front with his fellow?"

I participated in just such a recent major attempt at "rencontre." It was unique for the St. Louis area, one that has certainly not been spared the necessity for new forms of communication between black and white. The awareness was slow in coming. There has been some job opportunity, much private and public social leadership, and a residual aura of the long-gone Barnum Hotel where Dred Scott shined shoes in the shadow of the old courthouse in which he had once been pronounced chattel. Father Paul Reinert, the distinguished president of St. Louis University, and a great and sympathetic figure on the St. Louis scene, called the conference. Sensing the importance of the impending confrontation, not to him alone but to the whole community, he arranged it at the university's Fordyce House, a rural retreat. Under the title, *St. Louis in the Year 2000,* he arranged the conference in the hope that it would inspire the establishment of a permanent Urban Coalition in the St. Louis area. Nothing illustrates the breakdown in communication better than the pejorative secondary meanings that the term "urban coalition" has for some segments of the American community. Even something so well intentioned, necessary, in fact, long overdue, and under the guidance of one of the nation's most respected men, John Gardner, is dismissed out of mind by those who equate the term with concession to black militancy. Nothing could be further from the truth. It is a concession to nothing, and an acknowledgment of much that needs attention and change. Those who scorn the social worker approach, especially the governmental variety, should know the emphasis is on private initiative—private companies, private people. It provides a forum for people in urban communities who have never talked to each other before or, more importantly, listened. It is interesting in the light of the similarities between Latin and North American problems, to learn that John Gardner's replacement as head of the Urban Coalition is Jack Vaughn, former assistant secretary of state for Latin America and Peace Corps director. In any event, St. Louis needs a forum of this kind.

The whites know it. The blacks know it. Business knows it. Labor knows it. Still, against the backdrop of riots in other cities and church "drop-ins" in St. Louis, if it comes at all, it will be called something else. But it won't come to St. Louis if its advent depends on the kinds of awareness displayed at the first Fordyce Conference.

Attending were men and women certainly representing nearly every foundation block of the metropolitan "power" structure; industry, labor, university, church, municipal government, and foundation representatives were on hand, together with acknowledged leaders of the black community. The white participants included bewildered industrial leaders, reticent labor spokesmen, elected officials, and a few lay evangelists who like to stay two steps ahead of even the most whimsical black demand. Unfortunately, or fortunately, the complexity of the problem does not lend itself to the simple psychology of acquiescence. The blacks, too, represented a cross section of viewpoints as they would have to do, in a community so steeped in the tradition of apathy. Indeed, some of the more outspoken were relative newcomers to the St. Louis scene. But television and radio have long since lifted the ban on prophets from other countries. And the residents had been strangers to one another for a long time.

The invitees were the very people who, Father Reinert believed, could form a strong coalition framework. He had been unable to stimulate them individually by a circularized letter some time before. Responses, he said, were particularly slow from labor with the exception of the Teamsters' Harold Gibbons. By bringing them together under one roof to discuss the major problems confronting the community, Father Reinert hoped to weld, if not their views, at least their determination to find some common ground.

The group was divided into three committees, under the "American assembly" system. Each committee addressed itself to what its members identified as the five or ten most serious problems facing the area. They each began by agreeing, "The year 2000? Hell, let's look at St. Louis now!" Naturally, education, housing, and jobs won top recognition. "Law and order" was recognized as a serious problem, but one which grew out of a combination of educational failures, economic imbalances, and social unrest. The discussions were spirited. No one hung back. We found ourselves in a great deal of agreement on the priorities between us and the turn of the twenty-first century. The difficulty arose when we were attempting to synthesize our views into a consensus paper, which would serve to convey our conclusions to the public. It was at this point, apparently in each committee, that the black participants began to insist on prefatory language stigmatizing the white community for its "racism," and identifying racism as the key block to progress. Racism itself was not defined to anyone's precise satisfaction, but the entire report is infused with the term as if it had been. In my group I argued that a term normally shouted as a vilification should be used sparingly in any document intended to generate new and helpful attitudes in the white community, and stimulate its involvement in more effective joint efforts to raise the sights and standards of the St. Louis area poor. This paper was not intended to be a Sermon on the Mount, but an appeal to action. If the world were coming to an end, and this paper were to serve as a final pronouncement on what went wrong, there might be some justification for dwelling on this particular human weakness. But I could hardly believe that a generation of white entrepreneurs, as yet unmoved by the Bible readings, lectures, and preaching of decades, would suddenly find in this rather hastily drawn and semi-political document the way and the light out of the wilderness. On the contrary, I predicted they would receive it with the contempt a majority generally reserves for the morality of the minority.

I could only assume the paper would reinforce the psychology of confrontation, and in a way relieve the larger community from the burden of having to implement the otherwise reasonable recommendations of the document. On the other hand, I felt that the obvious economic and social defects of the area could be etched with sufficient clarity to touch the public conscience and get things moving.

The black participants disagreed. Those who wavered were easily brought into line at a later black caucus, and the final paper was drawn in black and white. It had the precise effect I predicted. It was rejected out of hand by those not already committed to the need for changes in attitude and opportunity.

One can speculate, of course, on the possibility that the paper received precisely the reaction the black participants wanted it to, that there was a higher value to them in letting fly these shafts, even though they would prove fatal to the cooperation needed. Those of us who are not black are frequently reminded we know nothing about how blacks think. I don't agree entirely, because a black is a man and therefore thinks like a man. Nevertheless, conceding the point, it is equally difficult for a black to think like a white, even though he may have felt obliged to simulate such awareness from time to time. There is one evident similarity between blacks and whites and that is that neither group responds sympathetically to moral lectures from the other.

Certainly the nation's responsiveness to racist "lectures" is limited, and to violence and the threat of violence even more so. Rebellion with the consent of the establishment is even harder to achieve than government with the consent of the governed. One lesson to draw from the failure of Fordyce has been long known to diplomacy. Kings mustn't meet too soon. It was a lesson in premature sum-mitry. Low level meetings should have preceded it. Talk-ing papers should have been prepared. All the participants should have been better briefed on the attitudes and terminologies they would encounter. Assaults on any Everest must begin with base camps.

CHAPTER SEVEN

America thrills to such big-top events as a moon landing. In a way they do bring us together because great glory like great tragedy seems personal to each of us. When smaller events, which affect the lesser known, are considered equally personal to each of us we will be even closer together. While I served in the Justice Department I read the following transcript of a recorded interview with two youngsters I never met.

Edward, age fourteen, a resident of the capital of the free world and described as "hopeless" by his school, was asked to tell about his life. He said,

Summers are the worst time. . . . drinking, cussing, stabbing people, having policemen running all around mostly every day in the summer time. In the winter time they don't come out because the whiskey store is closed, and then they can't have no argument, get drunk and start fighting.

Then he was asked what he would do if a TV camera came on his street. His reply:

I would like my neighborhood to be real nice, and not a whole lot of people be around there and fighting, fussing, police be always running around there. If they were making a movie around here, I would gather all the people up around on our street and tell them that "I would like to see y'all best manners when the studio came and film our street." So they come and we have our best manners and they film the picture and then show it. They'll say, that's a nice neighborhood. Then after that they'll forget all of their manners. All of the people will forget. They'll go back to drinking, cussing, fighting, shooting people, having policemen running all around on our street again.

Wendell, sixteen, a neighbor of Edward's, compared the neighborhood to the Maryland suburbs:

"I was being rode through Maryland once before. They has some pretty yards, you know, keep the yards clean. Here I guess the people don't care—when their children do something bad they don't bother with them. Then when they be drunk they beat them on the head. But if you raise children right, they'll be all right."

"When were you rode through Maryland, Wendell?"

"On my way to jail."

And so we leave "hopeless" Edward and Wendell-on-his-way-to-jail, wondering if, in time, the "events" of their lives will be considered personal to us all. Adult society should be particularly moved by their words, because they are not preaching. They are just "telling it like it is." How shall we show that we are listening, and that we have heard?

One way certainly is to insure that prisons offer opportunities for self-respect and self-renewal. So I visited the first one Wendell and Edward were likely to know—the Receiving Home—Washington's detention facility for delinquent and neglected youth. Some reception! Some home! There were ninety boys there—over twice the capacity. Cots were jammed together in the sleeping quarters. The younger boys were frequently assaulted by the older and threatened with worse if they reported it.

I asked the administrator what his principal need was. Another guard. Why? Because they had only one to check the seventeen-year olds' quarters. Often they grabbed him and took his keys. They needed another so they could work back to back. A reasonable request, I thought. It had been turned down by the House in an item-by-item survey of District welfare needs as transmitted by the former D.C. Commission. Extra guard? Why? The commissioners didn't know. No member of the House of Representatives had ever visited the Receiving Home at that time. With Solomon-like impartiality Congress could refuse both the chance to identify the problem and the money to meet it. At this writing the "Home" stands to be closed by court order for its patent inadequacies.

If it is clear we must do something to improve Wendell's new "home"; what about the old one, his neighborhood? We know there is work to do there, and we trust some of it is being done through programs of education, job training, and greater access to the proper public services of a civilized city. But there are quiet ways to subvert Wendell's world, and they should not be beyond the car or the reach of the law. I met his world when I accepted the case of a woman living in it who, after twenty years of payments, owned a ten-thousand-dollar house. Well-dressed callers representing the awesome Monarch Construction Company, since indicted, knocked at her door. They offered to improve the house by adding a "new-town front," aluminum siding to cover the old brick. Not to accept the offer, she was told, would be to subject the house to demolition by road builders. The cost would be a few hundred dollars and the contract was ready for signature. She signed. Shortly thereafter she received a payment book from a local bank. She had signed a note obligating a total payment of $8,000. I dug out the work permit from city records. It showed a materials estimate of $300. Then I called the bank and said that she would pay nothing, that in my view the bank had used the contractor as its agent in negotiating the note, that the signature on the note was procured by fraud imputable to the bank and actionable in triple damages. The lady heard little more from the bank. Months later, a call came to my home at night. It was one of the officers of the bank who asked somewhat plaintively if I "was still interested in the case." I assured him I was.

In 1966 when I went into Protocol I referred the case to a former law associate who rode it manfully out to the end. We were tempted to encourage the bank to sue on the note and then file a counteraction for punitive damages. But it would have been improper to induce the lady to go through the agonies of a trial merely to test our theory of the law. Her desire was to be relieved of an obligation she had not knowingly assumed. And she was.

I then received envelopes of scrawled petitions from neighbors of hers who had paid the money—or lost their homes. The scandal was lightly covered in the press, and legal action is still pending. But it is not difficult to understand how, to a neighborhood like Wendell's, the policeman is sometimes seen as the enforcer of laws that take rather than those that protect.

Wendell and his family have "met" their America through its con men and its cops. But many a con man and cop are under thirty as well as thousands of killed and wounded in Vietnam. Young Americans, be they junior achievers or junior under-achievers, heroes or escapists, require a clearer statement of America's goals if either their consent or their dissent, their involvement or their withdrawal, are to be worthy of the best in them.

In the meantime they must discover the practical utility of modesty and reserve in expressing their affirmation or denial of the notions and nostrums of our time. There are two reasons for this. First, overzealous commitments to error render orderly retreat from it awkward and time-consuming. Second, overzealous commitments to "truth" obscure the otherwise perceptible outlines of such truth. Zeal is innocence in action. But the purity of an idea can be stained by the vulgarity of its presentation. Our environment itself, the soiling of which arouses our righteous indignation, will not be cleansed until such indignation is reduced to reasoned cooperation. The attitude we bring to the discussion of great issues is the most important ingredient of our environment. Until this ingredient is refined we can confidently expect the other ingredients to remain unrefined.

In his first letter from summer camp, my son, then nine, observed, "The reason I haven't written you the names of my friends is I haven't got any." My daughter wrote in her first such letter, "I have made two friends, both of them dogs." The American child often arrives at the threshold of new schools, camps, and neighborhoods, with a certain sense of foreboding. But only this latest generation of American high school and college graduates has entered the larger world with that feeling. They would see more than humor in Bob Hope's advice at a commencement years ago. "To those of you who are going out into the world today," he said, "I have just one piece of advice, don't go."

But with rare exceptions, the past presumption of youth has been that somebody up there not only likes us, but legislates and governs for our benefit. Doubt has erased that dual presumption from today's young minds. Worse, the doubt itself has in some instances given way to the opposite view that the leaders of adult America are, in fact, not governing beneficially; and, rejecting that implication, resent any who raise it. Those who have raised it most noticeably are those who consider themselves most threatened by what they deem to be inadequate leadership. They are the young, because their lives are at stake. In fairness they are also concerned with more than that, with values beyond struggle, things of the spirit, humanity. A Harris opinion poll last year indicated that youth's disenchantment had origins not only in the current war but in a sense of lost or absent values, vague apprehensions they feel their parents do not share. We must recognize, although many of us do share those apprehensions, that from here on, we do in fact *share* them, that we are not in exclusive possession of them.

The Congress acknowledged that last year by extending the voting franchise to citizens between eighteen and twenty-one. The Supreme Court, testing how lively a "living instrument" the Constitution is, affirmed. The most cogent arguments favoring the statutory route were more political than legal. But continued denial of the franchise would also have had a more political than legal basis. This is certainly a forgivable inference to draw, particularly by those who have found themselves called on to defend "commitments" they have had no part in making.

During the House debate on the subject most opponents of the Voting Rights Act section conferring the vote on eighteen-year-olds voiced support of the *idea,* but opposition to the method. Fair enough, but would such tactical obstructionism have surfaced unless those opponents, speaking for themselves and their constituents, really questioned the political wisdom of the idea itself? In reply to one such member's suggestion that the Constitution was being sacrificed on the altar of political expediency, I said,

How can that be? Most of those who support the extension today face electorates this fall which do not contain one voter under twenty-one. How expedient is that? I would argue rather that thousands of young Americans in that disenfranchised age group have been sent to their final and untimely rest by authorities they had no political power to select or oppose. By that token hardly a corner of South Vietnam could not by now be considered an altar of political expediency.

In the meantime, whether we respect or distrust the opinions of young Americans, we should take care not to assume we can speak, much less think, for them. Nor should we use them to reflect our own biases. Their use of the franchise will reveal their own unity, their differences, and their confusion, as it has ours. Moreover, we should recognize that, unlike some other minorities, youth membership changes. A man is black for life, but eighteen for one year only. This year's crop of eighteen- to twenty-year-olds does contain many who think, speak, and act as if they expected to crowd a lifetime of commitment into one chaotic year.

In the wake of the original Cambodia announcement some three hundred high school and college undergraduates visited my office. They ranged in age from eighteen to twenty-one. They were quite familiar with the Constitutional provisions regarding the authority of Congress in matters of war. They wondered whether ,if the Congress were to close down and go home, there would be any perceptible change in national policies or any less control over them. Congress, I told them, was mulling that one over itself. At this writing it still is, although its efforts along these lines, even after ten years of undeclared war, are termed "interference" with Executive authority.

My visitors wondered further where their society was headed. They saw contrasts we did not even look for at their age. It is unnerving to them, in the din of official pronouncements concerning the preservation of freedom in Southeast Asia, missions flown, bombs dropped, and body counts, to learn of skinny peasants swearing eternal hostility to American imperialism. The enemy is not hate-ful enough to them nor the ally sufficiently lovable. Is our press to be scored for failing to make them so? We must remember that today's eighteen-year-old has seen the Vietnam war on the front page of the morning paper every day of every year since he was eight, with such intermittent promises of respite as the "home by Christmas" prediction of 1965. Those were years, also, in which he studied Amer-ican history, philosophy, and sociology, and tended quite naturally to discriminate between necessary and unneces-sary, if not just and unjust, wars. Contrasts abroad were no less vivid than those at home—which were preexisting but not unrelated by now. The American black and poor who would "always be with us" suddenly loomed into view as well as existence. So the young American of today is presented with an enemy he cannot hate, allies he cannot love, and fellow-citizens he doesn't know.

At fourteen, I was allowed to harness one of my grand-father's teams, hitch it to a cultivator, and cultivate corn.

Sitting on the swaying two-wheeler and talking to an
obedient team of horses gave me a grand feeling of control
and accomplishment. One afternoon a sudden summer
storm eclipsed the sun in seconds. A flash of lightning cut
across the dark sky, and the team bolted. I couldn't get
the cultivator's teeth up before we had torn up a whole
row of corn. In a driving rain we careened through the
gate, wheeled, and took off like Ben Hur's chariot. Moments later we clattered to a halt on the cobblestones of
the barnyard, and the team acted as bored as if nothing
had happened. At the first sign of danger they just decided
to go home. I knew I had no hand in our salvation.

Many young Americans today see their world being
pulled—to no safe refuge—rather to the brink of apoca-
lypse. They feel propelled by successive thrusts of mindless
self-interest through a vacuum of apathy with no one they
trust at the reins. They reflect this sense of futility in
predictable ways. Some leave, or dream of leaving, the
country for presumed havens of rationality and humanity;
others bid farewell not to our shores, but to the laws and
mores currently operative within them. I've met hundreds
of these youngsters, as well as many others headed for
tours of duty in Vietnam. One thing about the Vietnam
war, it has made us all think more keenly about the values
we send or surrender to it. Impulsive government tends to
rule an ever more contemplative people. The simple pas-
sage of time and the growing up of young sons to draft
age have had an effect on the attitudes of many families,
not so much toward patriotism itself as to the propriety of
spending it on the Fuller-brush fire wars of our time, sold
house-to-house and crowd-to-crowd by Presidential re-
minders of our historical purposes. The doubts raised are
not dispelled by candid admission on the part of President

Thieu that no South Vietnamese who has been jailed for political reasons may take further part in politics. Troubled by such nagging questions, the American adult, whether hard- or soft-hatted, has, nevertheless, reserved his principal resentment for those youth who resist or evade the draft, for others who encourage them to do so, and particularly for those who denigrate the flag and country as a way of expressing their opposition to the war. A regrettable corollary to such disrespect has been the tendency for many other Americans to equate patriotism with unequivocal support for our Indochina involvement —a tendency fostered in high places.

Avoiding the draft, on the other hand, by seeking educational privileges has been considered a reasonable course for the most patriotic of men: fathers who deem their sons' minds of greater national value than their trigger fingers. Many a deferred student seeks to atone for his privileged status by engaging in the politics of confrontation in opposition to the war. But there is no mistaking the intra-societal mistrust that is compounded by the disparity in educational opportunity. It is put into sharp relief by the irony of highly placed advice to universities to restrict their openings to "qualified" students. This, of course, would batten this escape hatch to those Americans who lack university credentials largely because their education up to that point has been below standard. Whether an all-volunteer army would cure or confirm this defect remains to be proven. Moreover, the "educated conscience" test for the nonreligious objector may do an injustice to the no less conscientious, if unsystematized, objections of the dropout or slow-witted.

Six years ago, as a Justice Department representative, I attended a high school conference in Los Angeles entitled

"Youth in Upheaval." (They had seen nothing yet.) The war was grinding on even then, and a number of youngsters said they would do anything to avoid involvement in it. One boy, sixteen, said, "I don't want to kill, and I don't want to get killed, but if my country asks me, I'll go." That the other boys were white, and he black, merely underscores the importance of looking to the man, not the collective, for a point of view.

Nevertheless, "I *don't* want to kill" remains a recurrent refrain in young America, black and white. And considering the criticism it attracts, it appears to be more a matter of found conscience than lost courage. It is the reemergence of that kind of primeval remorse Freud ascribed to man before civilization added "splendid little wars" and "body counts" to his parlance. On its face, as a desire, it certainly seems no more disturbing, let us say, than "I *do* want to kill."

David, a young man from a wealthy background in my home district in St. Louis County, stepped out of a picket line in front of the White House and called on me. He was a strong, fine-looking boy dressed in a field jacket and khaki trousers. "I don't want to kill," he said, as he sat, with folded hands, on the edge of the office chair. His father, a retired Army officer, still offered him room and board at home, but no money and no conversation. He was about to be drafted and wanted to talk with someone—his congressman would do. America's young, estranged from their parents, need "uncles" as never before. Many families are discovering they can counsel their friends' children more easily than their own. Representing fathers and sons who don't speak does give an added dimension to a congressman's job. In any case, I had spent much time advising youngsters concerning their choice of service, the reserve, etc. This boy needed counsel, too. I told him he seemed to be a conscientious objector.

"Yes," he said, "but it's more complicated than that. If I accept C.O. status I implicitly acknowledge the right of the Selective Service Board to send me to some noncombatant service and others to fight. I don't acknowledge that right."

I said the Selective Service was merely an instrument of government in this country during a dangerous time in an imperfect world. The world, he replied, was imperfect because people agree to kill. I asked him to tell me what he would do if a person approached him with a gun and threatened to shoot. He said he would tell the person, "I am no threat to you, but if you feel that I am, then shoot." He said that in that way the hostility would leave the killer, perhaps not in time to save him but others.

I reserved a doubt on that, and asked him then what he would do if he had loved ones with him when the killer appéared, loved ones for whom he bore the responsibility. He said he would talk to them about his decision, and let them make theirs.

"I mean children," I said.

He shifted in his chair. He would probably try to save them, he said. I told him then that I thought of the Nation as a kind of family, and that the province of Government was to remain in readiness to defend it, though reasonable men may differ on what would constitute necessary or prudent defense measures.

I recalled meeting Bertrand Russell after a *Herald Tribune* forum he addressed twenty years ago. I had asked Russell what would happen if the Western world took his advice—better Red than dead—and bowed to Communist totalitarianism. "A dark age would descend," he replied dreamily, "but a much shorter one than the last—perhaps not more than a hundred years. Their appetites fully satisfied, the aggressors would become more gentle and liberal. Their rigid regimes would evolve into something more tolerable. But if we were to oppose them now with our full might," he said, "we participate in the annihilation of the human race, and there's no comeback from that." Russell was consistent. In 1916 he had been dismissed from his lectureship at Trinity College, Cambridge, for a pamphlet he published critical of the Government's harsh treatment of draft dodgers.

It seemed to me and does now, I said to the young man, that Russell and he would gamble a hundred years of lives and dreams for an eternity of utopia which was no more than a figment of his imagination. "In effect you would sacrifice the dreams of your unborn children for your own."

"I understand what you are saying," he said, "but someone must begin the process."

"What can I give you," I said, "but cold comfort?" The laws of the Nation, which incidentally were the framework of his growth, schooling, safety, and progress to date, were not overly severe, "but you do face jail if you refuse to submit to the reasonable directives of the Government." Or, I said, he could leave the country—an alternative not open to the young dissidents of many other countries.

"I've thought of leaving," he said, "but I don't really know what I'll do."

To go to Canada, Sweden or some other so-called "neutral" place would be a false flight, I suggested. Both nations owe a portion of their stability to economic relations with us or other friends we support, and would surely look to us for political and even military assistance under certain exigencies. "You would feel silly at best, looking with Canadian apprehension for help from the America you abandoned."

"Yet if I go to jail," he said, "my life as an American will be forever stained. I will never be accepted again." That, I told him, was at the very core of his decision, the eaten cake. Like the Spartans at Thermopylae, Socrates, too, died "in obedience" to his country's law. Convicted of misleading youth he preferred the hemlock to flight because he would place only his principles, not his life, above the laws that gave Athens its structure and order. No one can expect to be fully accepted in his lifetime by the society whose laws he rejects while others die honoring them. But he could stay and work for change in a country where change can come from reason within and be defended from outside assaults.

We had talked for two hours. "One other thing," I told him, "I don't hate you."

"I know that," he said, "thanks."

How "rotten" was that apple of a young man? How much of a kook, misfit, effete, impudent snob? Was he less civilized than the rest of us? The thought occurred to me as the young man walked away down the corridor of clicking heels, miniskirts, and memoranda. This was before Cambodia and the Kent State tragedy. Our Laotian involvement, however, had just been revealed by the Senate subcomittee my father chaired. We had been promised a secret plan to end the war and presented with a secret war that could end the plan. The secrecy was justified, we were told, in that it permitted United States participation without embarrassment to Soviet Russia, a diplomatic nicety hardly reassuring to a society based on full disclosure and trust.

The "element of surprise" technique was then extended to Cambodia. The university delegations, which poured in, came from Haverford, Cornell, Princeton, Missouri, Washington University, N.Y.U., and Yale, but all from my district. They were informed, courteous, and puzzled. They declared the "system" unfit. I asked each group for a showing of hands of those knowing the name of their township or ward committeeman or woman, Republican or Democrat. Only once did a hand go up—with a question, "What are townships and wards?"

"Go home and see!" I advised, explaining they were political subdivisions where people got together to promote their ideas and candidates for government; in short —" the system." One young man had praise for the burners of R.O.T.C. buildings. "You might as well burn me," I replied, "because these institutions are the creations of law, and I help make the law. So you should get the source."

It was only a "symbol," he smiled. "No one was hurt."

I said that it seemed to me everyone is hurt when the law is broken. All over the world, from the nation's campuses and the still-gutted ghettos of Washington to villages in Indochina, burning is justified by the burners. Should "victory" go to the biggest torch bearer? The living, as Khrushchev said, would envy the dead. The young cannot wish that. And if he should succeed in toppling the system, I said, who would be the new Honcho? How would he be replaced if he proved unsatisfactory? And how would the obligations and functions of government be fulfilled?

"There will be time to consider that," he said, "when we get rid of what we have."

The Founding Fathers, I reminded him, spent much time speculating on what government should be before overthrowing the one they had—"a better approach than yours."

"You know what," said the young radical as he left; "I may vote for you."

Where, I wondered, had I failed? Perhaps he thought of me as the Indians did of Custer. It is said the Indians liked Custer because they at least knew where he stood.

CHAPTER EIGHT

Our sires begot the present race,
Of manners impious, bold, and base;
And yet, with crimes to us unknown,
Our sons shall mark the coming age their own.
——Horace, Ode VI to the Romans

We must certainly not cut and run from dialogue with the young. On the contrary we should seek it.

As members of the Science and Astronautics Committee, Congressman Ken Hechler and I were invited to President Nixon's state dinner for Neil Armstrong and his fellow-astronauts at Los Angeles' Century Plaza Hotel. When our cab neared the hotel we could see the front entrance was ringed by a thousand or more youngsters. Wearing ponchos and floppy hats they were chanting uncomplimentary things about the moon, the Government, and the police. The latter, not much older in appearance, were nervously fingering night sticks in a thin blue line. We knew that champagne would be served the guests and there were enough to drink it. We paid the cabby, and walked into the crowd. We were quickly spotted for our unconventional dress—black tie—and surrounded by a curious

throng. "What are you?" one asked. I told them that for
our sins we were congressmen from Missouri and West
Virginia. Then came the questions: Why the moon with
so much left to do on earth in housing, pollution, and
education? Why the war? Why germ warfare production?
Our first reaction was that these were not such bad questions. With one exception, at their age I had never asked
such questions.

In 1946, as an eighteen-year-old Marine private I was
waiting at Camp Lejeune for orders. Surrounded by
rumors of war in China, I wrote my grandfather, Congressman James Wadsworth of New York, "A little Chinese adventure would be a great way to end my tour, but tell me,
Gramp, are we at war with the Chinese communists, or are
the Marines just over there fighting battles on their own?"
I misplaced, and can't remember, his reply, but I'm confident it was reassuring. At any rate I assumed the folks in
Washington knew what they were doing. With Hitler and
Tojo conquered, what evils could remain? The only crisis
in my subsequent four years at Yale that brought the student body to the streets in protest arose when the Good
Humor man ran out of vanilla. The famed vanilla riot of
1948 was scorned by Harvard intelligentsia, which held a
mass rally that year for Pogo for President. In our case,
windows and heads were broken as the New Haven police
met their responsibility with gusto. But looking back I find
it difficult to equate either the vanilla cause or Pogo's
Presidential aspirations with the things that trouble today's youngsters.

So we answered the questions. President Nixon had just
announced the discontinuance of germ warfare production. Then, after the usual exchange about the wisdom of
our involvement in Vietnam and the difficulty of achieving

immaculate extraction, we went on to discuss space technology and its relevance to earthbound life: the weather satellites, which give advance warning of impending storms; the communications satellites, which can bring education and new knowledge into the remotest parts of the world; the earth resources satellites, whose infrared sensors may soon tell us far more about the subsurface of earth than we know today, telling farmers what and where to plant and fertilize and fishermen where the schools are headed, warning against overfishing or oil-drilling where the ocean's life cycle is threatened. Using this technique in foreign aid could give countries like India and Brazil more vital information in a week than a team of agronomists tramping through their fields and rice paddies could give them in a year.

We discussed other spin-off benefits: the pacemaker for heart patients, teflon-coated steel, the fire-resistant paint developed following the tragedy that took three lives. The very sight of earth as described earlier by Frank Borman gave us new perspective on its solitude. Like a spaceship the earth had its own life system that must not be compromised. Views of the earth's vital biosphere from space indicate the dangerous concentrations of pollution and the directions they take. In his book *Progress, Coexistence, and Intellectual Freedom*, the Soviet scientist Andrei Sakharov had predicted that at current and projected emission levels the United States and the Soviet Union might poison each other peacefully in thirty years' time with no hostile intent, a view echoed by United States witnesses before our committee. Such views from space underlined the importance of anticipating the secondary consequences of industrial growth and scientific experiment. They also point up the multi-disciplinary approach to the study of science and engineering that the universities will have to adopt if we are to graduate a generation of scientists with this new awareness.

As for man's curiosity about the universe, how was it, we wondered, to be limited or contained? Even in "failure" did we learn something about mankind. As Commander James Lovell and his colleagues calmly maneuvered their "lifeboat," the whole world watched that tiny struggle in the sky. Our earthbound problems seemed dwarfed for a moment by the uncertain fate of three Americans. What if on some future space platform American and Russian scientists can work together? Pierre Teilhard de Chardin's words, "things rising converge," could be true of the hopes of men.

Priorities, yes, very much so, and no one could argue a greater need today to seek microbes on Mars than health in our cities. But these were not concepts, I said, which were understood only by those under twenty-one. Mistaken we may be over thirty or over three, but not necessarily fools. Being young is no guarantee of being right. It merely provides the hope of outliving a few more mistakes.

The hour had gone. The young people thanked us and opened up a path to the door. Inside there were glitter, rhetoric, and tearful pride in the bravery, modesty, and achievement of three outstanding Americans and their patient, sacrificing wives. Yet I could not forget the youngsters outside. A letter from one of them expressed their gratitude for the chance to be heard. I came away with the impression that whatever they perceived to be true threats to this country they would resist.

Many educated young men of England in the 30's doubted any threat could warrant mobilization so soon after the Great War. It is well known that prior to the

Second World War student members of the prestigious Oxford Union voted overwhelmingly for the negative of the proposition: "Whether to fight for King and Country." In a few years many had been killed defending the affirmative. But they had to see it, to feel it, to believe it. Many young Americans today fail to discern such a test in Vietnam. To the contrary, the Armed Services report a near-drastic falling-off in career officer interest. And the questions are being asked early. I was told by the principal of one school that a newly arrived ninth grader soberly asked him if the school had any contracts with the Defense Department. "They usually just ask me the name of my dog," he said in wonderment. Other youngsters question the propriety of church confirmation at thirteen, when they can't even vote at eighteen. They are induced to decide on God, the greatest mystery of all, before country. If the existence of God were determined by vote, would they have to be twenty-one to participate?

If we all shared the same perceptions of danger, the principal remaining problem would be whether we were all right—or all wrong. In the meantime, action-oriented as youth are, they should recognize that action per se is not a substitute for knowledge. And being where the "action is" can be dangerous unless knowledge gets there first.

The Age of Aquarius is a questioning age. And we are as short of temper, at times, as we are of answers. Worse, we are tempted to attribute persistent challenge to the influence of subversive ideology, usually Marxism. Marx has adherents to be sure, but any flirtation with Marxism can only be brief for those who treasure human values. If the young American were to be asked, for example, what goals he would seek for his kind, he would quite likely include "justice, humanity, liberty, equality, brotherhood, and independence." What comfort would he derive in this regard from Marx?

Marx was as protectively sentimental about the Austro-Hungarian Empire as Hitler was about the Third Reich. In 1848 the Slavonic tribes in southern Europe demanded independence, and Mikhail Bakunin made an appeal on behalf of democratic panslavism with references to "justice, liberty and humanity." In 1849, the year after his *Manifesto,* Marx in collaboration with his colleague Friedrich Engels replied in a series of articles against panslavism, which were published in the *Neue rheinische Zeitung,* the following one on February 14, 1849 (taken from *The Russian Menace to Europe*):

"Justice," "Humanity," "Liberty," "Equality," "Brotherhood," "Independence"—so far we found in this panslavonic manifest nothing but these more or less moralistic categories which do indeed sound beautiful, but prove nothing in the field of historical or political questions. "Justice," "Humanity," "Freedom," etc., may demand this and may demand that over and over again; but if it cannot be done, then it is not going to be done and remains in spite of everything an "empty pipe dream."

Warming up to their subject, these two "liberal Communists" continued with the following revealing references to the Mexican war, a war which Lincoln opposed and Grant later branded as one of the most unjust ever waged by a democracy:

Will Mr. Bakunin reproach the Americans for a "war of conquest," which does give a bad jolt to this theory which is based on "Justice and Humanity," a war however which we know was made only in the interest of civilization? Or is it perhaps a misfortune, that the energetic Yankees . . . truly opened up the Pacific Ocean for civilization and for the third time in history gave world trade a new direction? The "Independence" of a new Californian Spaniards or of a few Texans may suffer by it, "Justice" and other moral principles may be here or there impaired; but what does that mean in the face of such historically important facts?

"Manifest destiny" could not have had more eloquent spokesmen. Imperialists, Marx and Engels believed what Jefferson was reluctant to believe, and Franklin firmly disbelieved, that there were inferior breeds of men whose paltry aspirations deserved to be crushed.

"There is not one country in Europe," wrote the founding fathers of modern communism,

which does not have in some corner or another one or several ethnic ruins. . . . Thus in Austria the panslavonic Yugoslavs which are nothing but the ethnic trash of a highly mixed-up thousand years old development. The fact that this equally mixed-up ethnic trash sees its salvation in the reversal of the entire European movement, which, as he sees it, should not move from West toward East but rather from East toward West, that for this ethnic trash the sword of liberation, the bond of unity is the Russian knout—that is the most natural thing in the world.

Attributed in large part to the pen of Engels the forgoing excerpts could hardly be disowned by apologists for his collaborator. Non-Russian Slavs have risen from the mire of Marxist contempt to revere its author as edited by the Russian knout. The paradox is not that the recent invaders of Hungary and Czechoslovakia claim to be Marxist, but that the victims do. What real comfort can be drawn from Marx's ethnic views by today's nationalism, the group humanism of our time, which accents the dignity of every race, every tribe, every man? Today where would Marx find work, never mind reverence? Having thus "met" its founder, we can lay to rest the notion that Marxism is or could be the inspiration for the humanistic, world-wide, student unrest today. We could even suggest worthier heroes for Russia herself, but she will happen on them one day, after rolling the stone back and forth from Stalin's grave a few more times. Nor should we deny the progress represented by the humane evolvement of Soviet policy toward dissident thinkers. Once silently eliminated, they are now audibly committed to mental institutions.

Their fathers as young men were engaged in an explosive challenge to autocracy that was actually nurtured by the emerging Bolshevik establishment, which scorned, then adopted, its autocratic method. The old people, the Uncle Tomskis of czarism, were publicly despised. It was a euphoric period for young propagandists for the new freedom, including for a brief time "liberated" women, often bald or topless, haranguing old ladies in babushkas about free love. The natural inclination of youth to challenge the past was well manipulated and exploited. Not far from the mark was Lichty's wry cartoon showing a little boy in a Russian shantytown proudly telling his friend, "Papa promise me gold watch if I do not denounce him to secret police before I am twenty-one."

The Orthodox Church, last refuge of the Czars, had to be humbled, the icons "clast," science revered. Young people were urged to visit a copy of the famous Foucault pendulum, which described a steady twenty-four-hour arc showing the earth's rotation as "natural," not God-made. The shriveled remains of "saints" were exhumed and strung up to prove that heavenward they did not go; and a cartoon mural of Lenin kicking a ball marked "truth" past the outstretched arms of God, the goalie of falsehood, was unveiled. Shortly after the First World War a pilot went aloft and returned to report "no sign of God," exactly as his countryman Titov did from an even higher vantage point a half century later. It is interesting to follow atheism's touching search for reassurance—this compulsion to justify disbelief and not simply "accept" it. The latter-day Christian emphasis on the "God within" as distinct from the "God above" would fare no better, being vulnerable to the refutation of Soviet surgeons and pathologists. Soviet advances in psychic research, however, must avoid encounters with an inexplicable intelligence.

In the meantime Russia has indeed looked to Karl Marx for the philosophic content of her system. Three generations of Soviet youngsters have studied Marx, the latest with the zest America's young reserve for the works of John Fenimore Cooper. It would be ironic, while young Soviet enthusiasm wanes, to find Marxist cults assuming leadership positions in Western youth and minority movements.

Once sanitized for Soviet consumption, no rebels with causes have bothered to look behind Marx's "Good Red Housekeeping seal of approval." To a lesser extent democracy's heroes have also been favored by selective inattention. One can point to the seldom published utterances of Lincoln and Jefferson doubting the innate equality of the African man. Such speculations by one of the nation's Founding Fathers and its savior are periodically resurrected by right-wing apologists to quiet uneasiness over conservative appointments, and by black anarchists to prove the intransigence of the white mentality. Lincoln's segregationist statements, like Judge Harrold Carswell's, were made in the heat of a political campaign. They prove he was for Union (and election) first, and perhaps not as "emancipated" as the egalitarians of today whose freedoms he died for. In retrospect, was he the wrong man for the job? And Jefferson, who believed the Indian the white man's equal, suggested that "given time" the black might be. Franklin, the old sage, had no doubts. The man, however, who gave his name to the durable "ism" that has anchored the hopes and rhetoric of a century of instant egalitarians, graded all races on a sliding scale from German on down. His opinion of Jews is faithfully reflected in Soviet policy today.

In the meantime, what has been built to date, especially in America, is due to the work of forebears whose energy and intelligence probably would not compare too unfavorably with that of today's youngsters. Some of the latter would tear it down. But, claiming a tolerance and sensitivity beyond our understanding, they must then be sympathetic to our skepticism concerning their unilateral right of demolition. We are no less concerned than they for the legacy we jointly prepare for unborn generations. Indeed, we can speculate that should the anarchic few develop tomorrow's institutions, they will jail more of their children than we. John Dewey, generally regarded as the father of progressive education, would hesitate to claim paternity to today's phenomenon of teacher intimidation and campus violence. In *Human Nature and Conduct* he agrees with Plutarch's observation that, "those who give rein to unworthy practices use an imaginary freedom to purchase a real dissatisfaction."

This has been amply demonstrated for us from Berkeley to Lamar. The speeches that preceded these and other events of our time prove that crowds are more easily brought to their feet than to their senses. Would that the loudest preferred to save than to slander their inheritance. They are a generation of politicians made possible by a generation of workers. They are bright, often brilliant, but not always intelligible. Two years ago in a crowded office, a number of younger congressmen, summer interns, and student leaders sat on the floor hugging their knees and looking solemn. Congressmen Ogden Reid and Allard Lowenstein had called the meeting to elicit a discussion, if not a pledge, of nonviolence by the student leaders in the upcoming school year. The Congressmen called on the students to speak first. And then it came—that stream of conscience and consciousness, which has caused a generation of fathers to barricade themselves behind their clichés. It moves up to the ceiling like the convoluted spirals, stars, and loop-the-loops of a Steinberg drawing. It produces sentences that couldn't be diagramed by a computer, paragraphs that in braille would sprain a man's hand. It was catching. Pretty soon we were all talking like that.

Surely the impasse is only temporary. When men speak the same language, and mean the same things by the terms they employ, emotion should not be a permanent bar to understanding. The problem of intra-American communication today is complicated by the tendency to foster departures from English. Among the pillars of the past that are being shaken, one must include the spoken word. We twist it and, surprised to find it useless, employ shouting, shoving, and other more primitive forms of communication. Even university students, concerned for the inner city, express that concern by adopting its most inflammatory slogans. "I have sworn," wrote Jefferson, "eternal hostility to every form of tyranny over the mind of man." The militant idiom of the street is a form of such tyranny, particularly if the society it threatens encourages it. If, unlike Churchill, we *demobilize* the English language, we have weakened the link between good resolves and good actions. To break a people, break its language. We have already begun by undermining the foundations of English. Latin and the classics are electives now. As I have said, in some grade schools teachers are encouraged to speak in the evolving jargon of the class. "Living English" and "real talk" are patronized. What can this mean for government, not to mention conversation, literature, character?

Only militant segregationists and black power advocates could derive any satisfaction from the failure of the schools to meet their first responsibility, which is to do away forever with the need for interpreters between Americans. What the guardians of division fear the most is that, while they are sleeping, people will cross no-man's land and speak with one another or, worse, share kindnesses.

I am sympathetic to the idea of national service, domestic and foreign, for all able-bodied Americans at eighteen, because from service to this country comes an understanding of its problems and its people. This in turn gives perspective to the yearning for change. Most of us can give help. We all need it.

CHAPTER NINE

I have mentioned the relevance of the Latin American experience to our North American cultural growth and prospects. It was underscored for me by a chance reference made at the summit conference of American heads of state at Punte del Este, Uruguay, in April, 1967. "May the genius of Uruguay, which produced *Ariel*, guide our thoughts," said Ecuador's President Otto Arosemena in opening the conference.

The Latins smiled. The Yankees studied their notes. After all, what was *Ariel*? I went into town and bought a copy.

Ariel is a touching and brilliant essay addressed to Uruguayan youth at the turn of this century. It urges them to revere the respect for truth of pagan Athens which early Christians refined with love of humanity, but which modern "democratic puritanism" was burying under layers of stifling conformity. *Ariel* saw the United States as "Caliban, a mighty confederation realizing over us a sort of moral conquest."

It cautioned young Uruguayans not to let admiration for North American greatness serve to "de-Latinize" them, or to weaken the *ultima Thule* of their identity. Its author, the "genius of Uruguay," was the writer Jose Enrique

Rodo. That Rodo is not known to us is unfortunate but understandable in the light of our general ignorance of Latin achievements in the humanities. Yet since we tend to expect a higher standard of alertness on the part of our professional observers than of ourselves, we can wonder why it was that no mention was made of this reference by any of the hundreds of perspiring North American reporters and newscasters, who ripped story after story off their typewriters, who thought the sessions anticlimactic after the "money figure" was confirmed, yet who haunted the hallways of the Hotel St. Raphael in search of "backgrounders." More remarkable is the omission in light of the fact that the reference was made in the *one* speech which in all other respects attracted the most attention because it departed from the general theme of mutual congratulations for jobs not yet done. The Alliance, in effect, said Arosemena, was not progressing, and Rodo, he implied, would have known why. A sketch of Rodo's work could have been provided by any Latin present. Paperback copies in Spanish were discoverable in the town library. Interpreters abounded. But *Ariel* was ignored for the same reason its gentle shafts have failed to dent the Anglo-Saxon consciousness, since they were fashioned and loosed seventy years ago. I am devoting space to this unknown critic because his genius merits it, and he said so well what Latins have felt so long. The loud society is impervious to all but shouting, and Rodo spoke in a natural tone of voice:

Any severe judgment formed upon our neighbors of the North should begin, like the courteous fencer, by lowering the rapier in salute to them. Easy is this for me. Failure to recognize their faults does not seem to me so insensate as to deny their qualities . . . the traces of their progress will never

be expunged from the annals of human right, because they
have been the first to evoke our modern ideal of liberty, and
to convert it from the uncertainty of experiment and the
visions of Utopia into imperishable bronze and living reality.

How lethal a thrust could follow such a cordial salute?
We should not be encouraged to remove mask and glove.
It was not for nothing that Rodo named the spirit of Latin
America "Ariel," and the utilitarian northern goals "the
goals of Caliban," saying

Orphaned of the profound tradition that attended his birth,
the North American has not yet replaced the inspiring ideality
of his past with any high unselfish conception of the future.
He lives for the immediate reality of the present, and for this
subordinates all his activities in the egoism of material well-
being albeit both indvidual and collective.

We, the harassed, taxpaying North Americans are the
masters, if not the slaves, of the reflex response to such
criticisms of our "way" of life, particularly when its pro-
ceeds are shared with our detractors. Yet by comparison
with some contemporary assessments of the American life
style by our own authors (Kenneth Galbraith, Norman
Mailer), Rodo's commentary is not severe. It is merely
pessimistic.

"The levelling by the middle class," he writes, "tends
ever, pressing with its desolating task, to plane down what
little remains of intelligentsia. The flowers are mown by
the machine when the weeds remain," and, "as Tocque-
ville had said, 'after the days of Jefferson and Hamilton
the Gods are disappearing.'"

Rodo feared "mediocrity" would engulf us, and that we
would be grateful. Such a compromise, he felt, was an
unworthy offering for the kings of American culture to

present to the newborn United States child, generation after generation.

If asked about the conquest of polio, malaria, and space, Rodo would acknowledge that "North Americans abound in fertile suggestions, profitable examples, inspiring admiration, astonishment, respect."

Or, as the Mexican, Paz, wrote a half century later, "They believe in hygiene, health, work and contentment, but perhaps they have never experienced true joy, which is an intoxication, a whirlwind."

Rodo had put it this way:

Nature has not granted them the genius for propaganda, the vocation of the apostle. They lack that great gift of amiability —likeableness in a lofty sense—that extraordinary power of sympathy with which those races endowed by Providence for the task of education know how to make of their culture a beauty, as did Greece, lovable, eternal.

What a rebuff to the good guys of the Western world! If we aren't amiable and likeable, what are we? Perhaps we confuse our knack of instant familiarity with the "amiability" of which Rodo speaks. As for our success at "propaganda" we can't help but show others what we raise to see better ourselves: the televised journey of an antacid pill through the mean national intestinal tract; the innumerable marquees glorifying our fathers and sons, the gunslingers. We propagandize inevitably well the sights and sounds of a Janus-faced society only the silent half of which rejects vulgarity consistently.

In North America, wrote Paz,

Men and women are subjected from childhood to an inexorable process of adaptation; certain principles, contained in brief formulas, are endlessly repeated by press, the radio, the churches and the schools. A person imprisoned by these schemes is like a plant in a flowerpot too small for it. He cannot grow or mature. This sort of conspiracy cannot help but provoke violent individual rebellions.

Voicing a typically European view, Rodo speaks, too, of "the solemn tone in which the North American utters the word 'art.'" He buys it, says Rodo,

to satisfy his vanity and acquisitive instinct, but he has never felt the divine frenzy of poem or picture. In such a surrounding, true art can only exist as the rebellion of an individual. Emerson and Poe are as misplaced fauna expelled from their original habitat by some geological catastrophe.

Rodo would agree that our science, technology, and marketing genius cooperate to give us a high standard of living. He asks, essentially, what is our high *reason* for living? We have answers, some more testy than persuasive. Nor may we shamelessly rely on what Santayana described as "that tiresome American thing, a joke," or any other glib substitute for thought. We work, earn, and provide for ourselves and others. But, of our "intensity of life," Rodo asks, "Has it an end that is worthwhile and a motive sufficient for its justification?"

We have only to recall his "courteous salute" to know that he well understands the "justification" we could offer. Yet he finds in us more sound than light. The latter, for Rodo, was the legacy of Athens, "whose very name pronounced illuminates for posterity an epoch of human thought, a horizon of history."

We trust our name will so shine, especially now that our flag juts stiffly from the moon. Rodo, in fact, wondered if we would "rewrite Genesis" and put ourselves "on the front page." He acknowledges a "lump in the throat" at the sight of the Statue of Liberty, but identifies more readily with the ancient traveler who "saw the rosy light of the marble and the sheen of Athena's spear over the early dawn on the Acropolis."

He is clearly after something beyond liberty, seeing liberty not as an end in itself, but as the essential means to a loftier search. He agrees with Goethe who "could say so profoundly that only he is worthy of liberty and life who can conquer it for himself each day." We demand liberty for less.

Yet we should be more grateful to the critic who expects too much of us than one who expects too little.

In the midst of Rodo's pessimism was hope. He looked forward to the day when our "gospel of rest and recreation," which he equated with the "otium" of the ancients, would include "any ideal concern, any object of meditation or study divorced from all relation to immediate utilitarian interest."

Now, two-thirds of a century later, in what meditations are we engaged in our "otium" at "prime" time? For every mind-stretching moment of sensitive reflection a hundred bullets and fifty fists crash into the world-made flesh, myriad sidelong glances welcome the magic of an uplifted arm, or confident smile, rendered odorless by modern science. The look of sweet surprise and laurels of laughter that once greeted the wit of Socrates are reserved now for hair that stays in place, and lotions that tan without burning. Violins and choral harmonies herald the arrival of a new toothpaste, or at a respectful distance support with swelling grandeur the mountain tryst of young lovers sharing the rapture of a new cigarette.

The entire panorama Rodo would consider "hazardous" to our spiritual health. He would certainly claim evidence that beauty here does not much exceed the depth of skin and that our "frenzy" for a deeper loveliness was not yet "divine."

He might discover that many who do not find intoxication in art, music, aesthetics, or philosophy, find it instead in alcohol, "speed," and other short cuts to nirvana. Life being choice, discipline declines. In Rodo's words,

In that society whose precept tends to put outside of what is obligatory the higher manifestations of abnegations and of virtue, practical considerations will always make the limits of obligation recede indefinitely.

Thus parental permissiveness becomes societal, and abstention from alcohol, marijuana, and pornography is no longer compelled. In the name of freeing the individual, society actually confirms his enslavement. Yet the post-school world still clings by a hair to "higher manifestations." Televised discussions in depth of philosophy or art as well as language and other instruction by low-voiced and dimly visible professors are available at 5 and 6 A.M. or on sparsely funded educational TV.

True, behind the sponsored cosmetic curtain, Rodo would still find the old concern for "equality" in the pursuit of the practical, and the lure of the limited:

A democracy, not subject to a superior instruction, not trained in liberal schools to the understanding of true human excellence, tends always to that abominable brutality of the majority.

The hegemony of excellence raised to power by natural selection was Rodo's prayerful hope for all democracies. What fair report could John Gardner, who shares and describes the same hopes, now give? Our progress in schooling did not go unnoticed. Rodo predicted of twen-tieth-century North America "that of all their struggle with ignornance the only gain will be a sort of semi-culture with a profound indifference to the higher."

"In case of a pinch," wrote John Dewey, "the masses prefer to be good fellows than good men." Feeling the pinch of self-generating materialism on the deeper nerve of conscience, we console ourselves and one another by being "good fellows" at home and abroad. André Malraux claimed man was a "fraternity joined in a drive to attain something beyond, outside himself." Rodo, too, believed "Antiquity had altars for the unknown Gods. Consecrate a part of your soul to the unknown future." Do we, can we, so consecrate? Or are we North Americans a people, as Santayana suggests in *The Last Puritan*, "who hate to think, who laugh at what people think, and respect only what people do . . . afraid of the truth"?

We'll answer for our values, we would reply. Let others scourged by disease, poverty, ignorance, and oligarchical political neglect, leaning on us for financial support, an-swer for theirs. No nation can swat a gadfly as thoroughly as we. One that has ceased to respond to swatting in lieu of other forms of communication is our own home-grown Ariel, the awakened spirit of black America.

"There is deep trust," wrote Rodo, "in Emerson's para-dox that every country on earth should be judged by its minorities and not its majorities."

Thus was a North American thought bounced off a Latin telstar three generations before the civil rights acts were passed. Rodo foresaw for the races

even a higher concord in the future, that will be due not to a one-sided imitation of one race by another, but to a reciprocity of influences and a skillful harmonizing of those attributes which make the peculiarities of either race.

To such a "higher concord" we should be committed. In the meantime how we are judged by our principal "minority" today is not an easy question. Who speaks for this minority? Is it a Sterling Tucker who declares, "We don't want their white middle class values," or a Bayard Rustin who assumes such values are precisely the goal of the black teenager who "wants to be part of the white-collar organization man's world that [as Rodo feared] is America's future, not trapped behind brooms and pushcarts." Rustin argues further that our society itself produced these yearnings when it "revelled in affluence, encouraged the consumption of trivia, and proclaimed the coming of computerized utopias," in the *New York Times Magazine* of August 13, 1967.

"If it is true," he writes, "that a Negro boy is nobody unless he owns alligator shoes and an alpaca sweater, who created these symbols? Who whetted this appetite? Who profited from the sale of these commodities, and who advertised them? And who is victimized?" Rustin is voicing the realization of Rodo's prediction that:

As fast as the utilitarian genius of the nation takes on a more defined character, franker, narrower yet, with the intoxication of material prosperity, so increases the impatience of its sons to spread it abroad.

Rodo would argue, moreover, that the white majority was victimized first. Is the goal of the heroic black struggle in North America, then, merely the right to *equal* victimization? Rustin sees the black irresistibly attracted to the flame that has long since consumed the larger society, and in *Dark Ghetto*, Kenneth Clark asserts without passion that the American Negro wants at least "the opportunity to reject" white middle-class values. But what about the present opportunity of the white community to reject its own lesser values? Is it more or less than that of a minority that has never shared them? Of which is the greater tolerance required?

The arrival of Americans, black and white, at this threshold of choice and perspective is a stroke of fortune. The tumult and the shouting die, the militant captains and kings depart, confrontation gives way to contemplation and a new awareness, and pride without prejudice can govern each man's choices. It is in this sense that Teilhard de Chardin's axiom that "things rising converge" has meaning for us. He saw evolution as the affirmation, not the negation of Christian belief. He would argue that the American soul will not be content to accept a silent place in a comfortable semi-culture "with a profound indifference to the higher." Higher understandings will converge.

A pre-Columbian legend tells of two eagles loosed from either pole and meeting at each one's limit of dominion. With primeval prescience the Indians of the Americas foresaw the future of their two continents. To one continent slaves were brought. In the other, slaves were found. In each, the descendants of each and of their masters have much to learn and teach in Rodo's spirit of "honorable emulation." "America," he wrote, "needs to maintain its original duality."

He was speaking of the whole family of American Republics. But within the United States alone there is an equivalent "coalition" as Rustin described "capable of exercising political power in the interest of new social policies," and, Rodo would add, new humanistic horizons. It has been suggested that the antidote for democracy is more of the same. A Poverty Program spokesman once

mentioned the need for the American black's application
to his problems of more "Christian pragmatism." This
utilitarian principle Rodo would cautiously admire, but
not at the expense of what the official is said to have be-
littled as "black romanticism."

Our society needs both. And perhaps it has sacrificed
enough romanticism on the altar of pragmatism. Losing
touch with one's own unknown Gods does not entitle one
to invite, much less require, others to do so. A great race
of people might well prefer to be reduced to its last puritan
than its last romantic. In the duality is the cementing
strength. Meanwhile our take-a-bath and get-a-job admoni-
tions to the currently noncompetitive at home and abroad
reflect an honest distaste for dirtiness and laziness as we
understand those terms. But in other's eyes dirty is he,
however well scrubbed, who would profit from dehuman-
izing his fellow-man, and lazy is he who will not ask himself if this is happening.

One can at least believe in original innocence. Youth
should be urged to preserve as much of that residue as possible against hokum and harangue and refuse to elevate
the purveyors of either into power or prominence. Of
course, many young people get to be rather good at hokum
and harangue themselves. Nor has power per se proven
distasteful to them. Others, barefoot and beflowered, wan-
der the streets and gather at establishment happenings to
remind the over-thirty generation of—what? Their dissatisfaction? We share it. They have no corner on love, hate
—or, indeed, honesty. As a society we will simply have to
continue educating one another, young and old.

Plutarch gave us this Latin lesson: "They alone live as
they will who have learned what they ought to will." Another Latin stranger gave it again before the Panama

Canal treaty was negotiated, or Fords were driven, or airplanes flew. Rodo remains a stranger, but a patient one. He wrote:

Can you not picture to yourselves the America we others dream of? Hospitable to things of the spirit, and not only to immigrant throngs; thoughtful, without sacrificing its energy of action; serene and strong and withal full of generous enthusiasm; resplendent with the charm of morning calm like the smile of a waking infant, yet with the light of awakening thought. Think on her at least; the honour of your future history depends on your keeping constantly before your eyes the vision of *that* America, radiant above the realities of the present like the rose window above the dark nave of a cathedral.

This vision of the Americas should have a claim on us all at least as vivid as those of coffee, sugar, cocoa, bananas, oil, dollars, and jet fighters. If we could together follow that gleam, consecrate ourselves to that radiant future, how different might be our response to the nagging challenges of the present, how much more sensitively careful our preparation of alternatives to violence, and how candid our conversations. Latin American scholars can be misread. But they deserve to be read.

Of course, ripostes can be made to our Latin "teachers." Events render some of their judgments out of date. Nor can they or we "romance" ourselves out of poverty and hunger. But a society as young as ours, growing fast on the foundations Rodo so well defined, must be careful not to think it has outgrown them, or that speed of growth per se guarantees a good direction. A case can be made for postponing the search for "beauty" and "truth" until basic political freedoms and economic progress have been established. Latins might dispute this, but the important fact of Latin

America is that the intellectual and artistic community itself has always been in the forefront of democratic reform movements.

In his appearance before a joint session of Congress, President Díaz Ordaz of Mexico mentioned "goodness" as the "noblest of sentiments" in the fulfillment of freedom and social justice. In support he noted Henry Thoreau's remark that "goodness is the only investment that never fails." This would sound trite and evasive from an American politician. "Goodness" means both too much and too little. Too little in that it is not specific; equality, opportunity—those are the "goodnesses" we "know." But to ask more for "goodness" sake is to ask too much. Priests and ministers may be forgiven the question within church walls; but not strangers, teachers, or officials. The only candidate in the frenetic elections of 1968 even to mention the "*good* society" was Norman Mailer. I was about to add "curiously enough," but no—Mailer lost, came in fourth out of five, is a writer not a politician, is a liver of life not an orderer of lives. So it is not so curious that he of all candidates could define the "good society," the government of which would place the "fewest impediments in the way of people developing themselves."

But anyone present a year earlier on the occasion of Díaz Ordaz' address before the joint session would have seen enough boyish faces in the audience, the faces of pages and staff assistants filling the seats of absent legislators, to know how interested our politicians were in the message of a Latin leader. "Intoxication" remains a martini, the "divine frenzy" a Negro revival meeting, and "goodness" Mom's apple pie. It is a time, not for greatness (let's be modest) but for goodness. We know a society is not great merely because it is big, or loud. It is great if it can listen. The web of the listening society has a tensile strength. It can't be pulled apart as long as the stirrings of human aspiration can be felt in every corner. If it stiffens, it needn't be pulled apart; it will break apart. The society that listens is finally able to meet and be met. How grateful should we be, then, for gentler voices, its own, and those of neighbors, which would both stretch and strengthen what Lincoln called our "mystic chords of memory." As fellow-descendants of discovery, we should help each other pioneer the higher understandings, which wait to be found in the shared and friendly environment of this hemisphere. In his essay, "We Must Save Mankind," Teilhard de Chardin concludes:

Scattered throughout the apparently hostile masses which are fighting each other, there are elements everywhere which are only waiting for a shock in order to re-orientate themselves and unite. All that is needed is that the right ray of light should fall upon these men as upon a cloud of particles.

Ariel closes with the same hope:

See . . . while the crowd goes by, it never looks up to the heavens; yet they look down upon the multitude. . . . something descends upon the indifferent mass. . . . the vibration of the stars reminds me of the waving arms of a sower, sowing seed.

A man has a choice. He may become part of the "indifferent mass" or he can be a sower of seed. Nations, too, can choose. Two centuries ago we chose to be sowers of seed.